Cambridge Elements ☰

Elements in Politics and Society in Southeast Asia
edited by
Edward Aspinall
Australian National University
Meredith L. Weiss
University at Albany, SUNY

ISLAM AND POLITICAL POWER IN INDONESIA AND MALAYSIA

The Role of Tarbiyah and Dakwah in the Evolution of Islamism

Joseph Chinyong Liow
Nanyang Technological University

CAMBRIDGE
UNIVERSITY PRESS

Shaftesbury Road, Cambridge CB2 8EA, United Kingdom

One Liberty Plaza, 20th Floor, New York, NY 10006, USA

477 Williamstown Road, Port Melbourne, VIC 3207, Australia

314–321, 3rd Floor, Plot 3, Splendor Forum, Jasola District Centre,
New Delhi – 110025, India

103 Penang Road, #05–06/07, Visioncrest Commercial, Singapore 238467

Cambridge University Press is part of Cambridge University Press & Assessment,
a department of the University of Cambridge.

We share the University's mission to contribute to society through the pursuit of
education, learning and research at the highest international levels of excellence.

www.cambridge.org
Information on this title: www.cambridge.org/9781108705585

DOI: 10.1017/9781108669047

First published 2022

A catalogue record for this publication is available from the British Library.

ISBN 978-1-108-70558-5 Paperback
ISSN 2515-2998 (online)
ISSN 2515-298X (print)

Islam and Political Power in Indonesia and Malaysia

The Role of Tarbiyah and Dakwah in the Evolution of Islamism

Elements in Politics and Society in Southeast Asia

DOI: 10.1017/9781108669047
First published online: August 2022

Joseph Chinyong Liow
Nanyang Technological University

Author for correspondence: Joseph Chinyong Liow, iscyliow@ntu.edu.sg

Abstract: Islamism in Indonesia and Malaysia has undergone a fascinating transformation from its social movement roots to mainstream politics. How did this take place, and to what ends? Drawing on social movement theories, this Element explains the transformation by focusing on key Islamic social movements in these two countries. It argues, first, that the popularity and appeal of Islamism in Indonesia and Malaysia cannot be understood without appreciating how these social movements have enabled and facilitated mobilization; and, second, that it is precisely these roots in civil societal mobilization that account for the enduring influence of Islamist politics, evident in how Islamic social movements have shaped and transformed the political landscape. These arguments will be developed by unpacking how Islamist ideas took root in social movement settings, the kinds of institutional and organizational structures through which these ideas were advanced, and the changing political landscape that facilitated these processes.

Keywords: political Islam, social movement, Islam, Indonesia, Malaysia

ISBNs: 9781108705585 (PB), 9781108669047 (OC)
ISSNs: 2515-2998 (online), 2515-298X (print)

Contents

1 Introduction

Notwithstanding the publication of several seminal studies focused on Southeast Asia, there remains an inherent bias in the literature, where scholarship on Islamist movements tends to be dominated and shaped by analytical frameworks and historical developments that have emerged from the Middle East and North Africa. The most recent iteration of this was the "Arab Spring" and its aftermath, which witnessed something of an apex of Islamist activism, as Muslim political opposition and civil society groups joined forces in mass protests – some violent, but many peaceful – that overthrew dictatorships in Egypt and Tunisia and catalyzed widespread demonstrations in Algeria, Bahrain, Lebanon, Jordan, Kuwait, and several other countries, which were forcefully suppressed. Perhaps the most devastating consequences were seen in Yemen, Iraq, and Syria, where protests eventually escalated into full-blown civil wars and insurgencies that in their most extreme form gave rise to the brutal Islamic State terrorist movement. Indeed, the "Arab Spring," and the "Arab Winter" that followed soon after, has provided a treasure trove of data for scholars hoping to advance our current understanding of how and why Islamists mobilize, the degree to which such efforts succeeded in some cases but failed in others, and – at a more theoretical level – the compatibility of democracy with Islam (Hamid Dabashi 2012; Danahar 2013; Grand 2014; Worth 2015; Hafez Ghanem 2016; Baczko et al. 2018).

At the same time, this bias has also somewhat obscured the role that South Asian Islam has played in shaping developments in Southeast Asia since the early 1920s. Indeed, Muslim scholars from South Asia have never considered themselves to be on the periphery of the Islamic world, nor did they assume they were subservient to their counterparts in the Middle East. This greatly aroused the curiosity of scholars of Islam in Southeast Asia as they began to refer to works being transmitted from South Asia. South Asian Islamic intellectuals felt sufficiently authoritative to comment on a host of legal, sociopolitical, and religious issues, and these opinions were actively published and circulated both in South Asia and beyond the region (Mohd Kamal Hassan 2003; Pernau 2003).[1]

Of late, more attention has been shifting to Europe in the search for fertile empirical and analytical soil for the study of Muslim mobilization. Again, much of this scholarly interest has been prompted by high-profile events, such as

---

[1] Pernau mentions the print war that had developed in nineteenth-century India, which seemed to have developed across South Asia, with Islamic thinkers of the time engaging in polemics and printing various articles and pamphlets to articulate their positions on various individuals and issues. Islamic intellectuals in Southeast Asia were drawing heavily from the works of their South Asian counterparts.

several incidents of religiously inspired terrorism that took place in London, Paris, and Madrid after the tragic events of September 11. These events have occasioned greater interest in Islam and its engagement with mainstream European society and politics; here, however, the points of inquiry tend to revolve around questions of minority identity and the status of European Muslims in terms of their social and cultural integration into non-Muslim societies, whereas in the case of North Africa and the Middle East, it is very much about shaping the politics of the Muslim-majority countries in those regions. Compared to what has happened in these other regions (not to mention Iran and Turkey as well), interest in the terms and outcomes of Islamist political engagement in Southeast Asia in recent years has, for the most part, attracted relatively less serious systematic scholarly attention. This belies the fact that Islamism in Southeast Asia has undergone a fascinating transformation in the last two decades.

1.1 Why Southeast Asia?

Approximately 14 percent of the global Muslim population resides in Southeast Asia. The region is home to the most populous Muslim country in the world, Indonesia, also one of the largest democracies in the world, which incidentally supplies the largest contingent to the annual Haj pilgrimage each year (around 200,000 pilgrims). Malaysia and the Sultanate of Brunei are two other Muslim-majority countries in a Southeast Asia that also boasts sizable Muslim minorities in Singapore, Thailand, Myanmar, and the Philippines.

Geographically removed from the Islamic "heartland" of the Arabian Peninsula, Southeast Asia's interactions with Islam have historically been complex and dynamic, involving the localization of various aspects of the religion and its integration into the cultures and communal identities in the region. Correspondingly, a notable volume of scholarship (much of it distinct from the literature on Islamism) has been produced documenting the rich cultural inheritance and diverse historical tapestry of Southeast Asian Islam, in many ways unique to the Indo-Malay archipelago (Fealy and Hooker 2006). With regard to the hegemonic dominance of Islamic ideas and thought emanating from the Middle East and South Asia, it is worth mentioning that Southeast Asian Islam also enjoys a long, albeit somewhat overlooked, intellectual tradition of its own. Prominent Southeast Asian scholars, popularly known as Ulama Jawi, sojourned, studied, and taught in the storied *halqah* (study circles) of Masjid al-Haram in Mecca in the nineteenth and early twentieth centuries. These included Daud Abdullah Fathoni and Zayn-al-Abidin Fathoni of Patani, Muhammad Yusuf Ahmad (more affectionately known as Tok Kenali) of

Kelantan, Muhammad al-Nawawi-al-Jawi of Banten (Shaykh Nawawi Banten), and Agbdul Halim Hassan of Binjai (Tagliacozzo 2009). This tradition of scholarship flowed into the modern era through the works of renowned Indonesian scholars of Islam such as Nurcholish Madjid, Abdurrahman Wahid, and Syafii Ma'arif and Malaysian counterparts such as Nik Aziz Nik Mat and Ishak Baharom. Indeed, Southeast Asian Muslims have always had among their ranks thinkers and scholars who have made major contributions to the body of Islamic knowledge.

Against the backdrop of this vibrant Islamic culture and intellectual tradition, the last few decades have witnessed Islam assume greater importance in society and politics, accompanied by an upsurge in piety and religiosity across Southeast Asian communities in general.[2] Whether we consider the rise and growing popularity of Muslim political parties, the wave of popular protests against the USA during the turbulent era of the global war on terror, the introduction of the *hudud* penal code in Brunei, or the mass mobilization during the Jakarta gubernatorial elections, Islamic activism in Southeast Asia has undergone a fascinating transformation even as Muslim political mobilization and engagement is increasing across the region. This transformation is also evident in how Muslim social movements are increasingly engaging and collaborating with Islamist parties, even as these parties themselves appear to have evolved from their reformist, civil society activism roots as social movements to assume greater prominence as mainstream political actors. Underpinning this evolution is a belief, held in many quarters in the vast and diverse Muslim populations across the region, that Islam is not just a religion but a foundational organizing principle for modern society from which political leaders, parties, and organizations can derive legitimacy and authority. In other words, in these quarters, piety is increasingly finding expression as political ideology, or Islamism.

This is not to suggest though, that Islamist parties are on the verge of coming into power, or that Islamist regimes will be mushrooming across Muslim Southeast Asia anytime soon. Indeed, this is a peculiar paradox, for there are compelling reasons why this is not likely to happen. Nevertheless, as the following discussion of Indonesia and Malaysia illustrates, the reality remains that while prospects of Islamists being conveyed into political power on their own effort through the electoral process remain remote for various historical and structural reasons, their ability to shape national politics in these two countries will nevertheless continue to expand. It is this latter phenomenon that informs this Element.

---

[2] Oft-cited evidence of this includes the popularity of the Islamic headscarf, expansion of mosque construction (much of it funded by Saudi Arabia and Gulf states), the growth of the halal food industry, and the expansion of Islamic education through the proliferation of both public and private Islamic schools and institutions.

1.2 Arguments and Structure

By way of the above observations as a point of entry, this Element proposes to better understand the dynamics of Islamist mobilization in Southeast Asia by considering several questions. What are the Islamist signifiers, by which we mean, in essence, the intellectual and conceptual foundations in terms of ideas and ideals that underpin mobilization, and why do they resonate? How has the relationship between Muslim social movements and political parties evolved in terms of organizations and networks through which their mutually imbricated interests and identities intersect and interact, and equally important, the organizational capacities that reinforce and deepen these linkages? What role has the wider social and political context to play in framing the narrative of Islamism in Southeast Asia and providing the conditions for Islamist activism to thrive in the region? This Element will attempt to explore these questions by focusing on Tarbiyah and Dakwah as social movements, and their relationship with Islamist political parties in the Indonesian and Malaysian landscape.[3] A primary contention advanced here is that the popularity and appeal of Islamism in Indonesia and Malaysia today cannot be understood without first appreciating how these social movements have enabled and facilitated mobilization. In both Indonesia and Malaysia, Islamist social movements such as Tarbiyah and Dakwah, like many of their counterparts elsewhere in the Muslim world, germinated ideas, marshaled resources, and mobilized outside of formal political channels, forming the foundation upon which later political activism would be built. Yet, whereas coterminous social movements such as the Ikhwanul Muslimin (Muslim Brotherhood) in Egypt enjoyed only a short-lived foray into mainstream politics before being unceremoniously removed from power, in Indonesia and Malaysia Islamist social movements – that is to say, Islamic social movements that consciously assume a political character at some point in their development – would permeate, shape, and ultimately transform the mainstream political sphere.[4] Therein lies the point of departure of this Element insofar as the study of Islamist social movements and political activism is concerned, and it is not an incidental one. Because of their roots in civil and

---

[3]   This Element uses Tarbiyah and Dakwah to refer to two Islamist social movements, as they have come to be known, that emerged in Indonesia and Malaysia respectively. Where *tarbiyah* and *dakwah* are used in the text, they refer to Islamic education and Islamic proselytization respectively (and not the social movements).

[4]   Following the downfall of the Hosni Mubarak regime in February 2011, the Ikhwanul Muslimin formed a political party, the Freedom and Justice Party, and proceeded to dominate parliamentary elections that were conducted in phases between November 2011 and February 2012. The Ikhwan's presidential candidate, Mohammed Morsi, became Egypt's first democratically elected president after he won the second round of the presidential election in June 2012. He would be removed from office after barely a year, via a coup in July 2013.

political activism, Islamist social movements can have – and have had – decisive influence on Islamist politics; and, depending on the conditions, this influence is not only enduring but can also transform the political landscape.

The analysis that follows will make these arguments by investigating the interaction between the signifiers that underpin Islamism as it has evolved in these two countries and the roles they play in catalyzing engagement and activism, the organizational structures and networks of these social movements and affiliated political parties as well as the relationship between movements and parties that these dynamics have generated, and the wider context of the political landscape in which they exist and operate. Because of the large number of activist civil society collectives that populate the Islamic social movement landscape in Indonesia and Malaysia, including several that were creations of the state or that have evolved to be closely aligned with it, it would be impossible in this brief study to provide exhaustive coverage of this kaleidoscopic terrain. As such, while this Element will treat Tarbiyah and Dakwah as social movements and also make reference to a range of groups and organizations associated with them, for purposes of deeper analysis, it will focus more closely on more influential organizational expressions of these movements. Hence, in the case of Tarbiyah in Indonesia, analytical attention will center on organizations such as Dewan Dakwah Islam Indonesia (DDII; Indonesian Islamic Propagation Council) and Partai Keadilan Sejahtera (PKS; Prosperous Justice Party), while in Malaysia, it will be key Dakwah-linked organizations such as Angkatan Belia Islam Malaysia (ABIM; the Malaysian Islamic Youth Movement), Islamic Representative Council (IRC), and Parti Islam Se-Malaysia (PAS; the Pan-Malaysian Islamic Party).

In focusing on Tarbiyah in Indonesia and Dakwah in Malaysia, this study acknowledges the existence of key differences, especially in the structure of these movements. For instance, while Tarbiyah was arguably more amorphous as a movement, in the sense that it did not revolve around any major formal organization(s), Dakwah essentially found expression in the formation and activism of a number of Islamic civil society collectives of various stripes and ideological inclinations, some as extensions of the Malaysian state and others in opposition to it. This study also recognizes that the Tarbiyah and Dakwah movements in Indonesia and Malaysia were hardly monolithic; they comprised different streams of thought that were expressed in different institutional forms – some more cultural in orientation and others more political. At the same time, the Element has chosen to focus primarily on Tarbiyah and Dakwah for four reasons. First, although they might differ in terms of how they are expressed organizationally, both are mass movements that eventually adopted a political program. Second, their ideas and mobilizational capacities as social movements have evolved over time and taken on a decisively political flavor, in the process shaping the prevailing views of Islamist social movements writ large. Third, these movements are represented in part or in whole by collectives that exist outside of the state structure and that engaged mainstream politics from that vantage, even though at some point some participants became imbricated with or part of the state apparatus. Finally, while the Tarbiyah and Dakwah movements are admittedly defined by a rich diversity, this study is expressly interested in – and will primarily focus on – those aspects that have found political expression through their discursive ideas, institutional character, or mobilization activities. In other words, this Element is concerned chiefly with features of Tarbiyah and Dakwah mobilization and activism as pressure groups that advocated a political agenda (thereby explaining their "Islamist" nature and character). Notwithstanding this primary focus on Tarbiyah and Dakwah, the discussion will touch on similar movements when the opportunity arises.

2 Unpacking Islamism, Social Activism, and Politics

It is important to clarify a few things about Islamism at the outset. Understood as an ideology that calls for society to be organized on religious principles drawn from Islamic holy scriptures and the collective body of Islamic thought, the concept of Islamism has been the subject of extensive theoretical and analytical inquiry since the early 1970s, when scholars observed a series of high-profile events in the Middle East that involved social and political activism undertaken by Muslims. Events such as the Arab–Israeli War, the Soviet invasion of Afghanistan, the Iranian Revolution, the assassination of Anwar Sadat in Egypt, the Hamas uprising in Syria, the Palestinian Intifada, and several others witnessed the collective mobilization of groups of individuals, many of whom responded to the call to action made with reference to Islamic causes, symbols, and traditions. What stood out from accounts of these events was the prevalence of the use of religion – Islam – as both narrative and signifier on the part of those who participated in them. Concomitantly, these developments would spawn a cottage industry of scholarship that sought to understand how Muslims used – and responded to – religion in their agitation for social, political, and economic change. A Muslim middle-class intelligentsia soon emerged to propagate a political ideology of "Islamism" that would underpin a political project known in the contemporary parlance as "political Islam" (Fouad Ajami 1981).

On the face of it, Islamism appears to possess a master narrative predicated on several unifying themes. In its essence, Islamism is a revolutionary political ideology centered on an interpretation of Islam that calls for social and political engagement (as opposed to private religion) toward the ends of liberating and uniting the *ummah* under the banner of a state governed by Islamic law. A historical feature of Islamism is its emergence from the cauldron of the Cold War as an expression of anti-imperialism. By this token, advocates of Islamism have understood it as a rejection of Western "modernity" in favor of the "pristine" or "authentic" Islam that was practiced at its founding, although others have rightly pointed out that Islamist discourse could just as well be a product of modernity, at least in terms of its statist orientation (Halliday 2005).

At the same time, observers have on occasion a tendency to conceptually parse Islamism by controversially (and sometimes problematically, from an analytical perspective) prefixing the term with adjectives such as "radical," "fundamentalist," and "militant," according to how accommodating the political beliefs of Islamists are and the methods through which they seek to advance them. Indeed, care should be taken to stress that while such labels do to some extent reflect the reality that Islamism is an ideology that encompasses a diverse body of adherents and repertoires of engagement rather than a monolithic and uniform set of ideas, they still tend to essentialize and straitjacket an otherwise-dynamic sociopolitical phenomenon that does not lend itself easily to strict typologies. By way of illustration, it would be quite conceivable for an Islamist group to be, at once, "radical" in its rejection of the prevailing appeal of modernity, as well as "fundamentalist" on the grounds that their opposition to modernity finds expression in a call for a return to an imagined pristine, unvarnished Islamic past.

In keeping with conceptual discussion of Islamism, it is worth considering its correlation to strict, literalist variants of Islam known as Wahhabism or Salafism. While some Salafist and Wahhabist advocates of Islamism undoubtedly exist, there are others who in fact eschew political engagement, even though their views on social matters are incompatible with those upheld by the nation-state of which they are citizens, preferring instead to acquiesce with or dissociate themselves from the sphere of politics. In the same vein, there are Islamists who would not be considered literalists but traditionalists, in that they follow the orthodox schools of Sunni Islam that Wahhabis and Salafis shun as innovations (*bid'a*).

While Islamism is a distinct political project, some scholars have attempted a broader definition of Islamism to encompass activities beyond political engagement. For instance, Salwa Ismail suggests that Islamism is not only about politics but also "re-Islamization, the process whereby various domains of social life are invested with signs and symbols associated with Islamic cultural traditions ... [It] is not just an expression of a political project; it also covers the invocation of frames with an Islamic referent in social and cultural spheres" (Salwa Ismail 2003: 2). There are two problems with broadening the definitional parameters in this manner. First, contending that political Islam looks beyond politics and covers cultural expressions in various domains of everyday life essentially makes every practicing Muslim ipso facto an Islamist, that is, an advocate of Islamism, or at least potentially one. This clearly cannot be the case. Second, the obvious reality would also be that not every devout Muslim desires social or political change or feels any responsibility or obligation (as a believer) to agitate for it. In fact, some Muslims might oppose outright the Islamist agenda of introducing Islam into the corridors of power. This is not to say that a broader conception is of little utility, particularly if we are concerned about enabling environments that give rise to Islamism. Rather, the point to stress is that in order to generate analytical traction and maintain conceptual precision, it is best to remain focused on the essence of Islamism in terms of manifestly political acts and the political motivations behind them. A broader conception is useful only insofar as it illuminates how the wider environment facilitates such politicization of Islamic identity and consciousness. At any rate, that social movements are usually described as networks of individuals and groups engaged in collective action in pursuit of social change on an issue that affects a society means that they are, by definition, already political in both nature and expression (Diani 1992).

2.1 Islamist Signifiers

Social and political action are not simply manifestations of behavior, for this behavior must be understood in context and categories that provide the meaning and intelligibility that underpin them. It is in this respect that studying Islamist activism requires an understanding of its signifiers, understood as the ideas, ideals, and symbols that frame mobilization.

The signal idea Islamists of all stripes (or passports) propagate would be the Islamic state. Not to be confused with the Iraq- and Syria-based terrorist organization, Islamic State of Iraq and as-Sham or ISIS, the Islamic state essentially encapsulates the notion that a sovereign state should be governed by Islam, such that the state would derive the law of the land primarily, if not exclusively, from Islamic teachings. In other words, Islamists aspire to seize political power through which they can shape, if not control, the government toward the ends of creating an Islamic legal, social, and political order that finds ultimate expression in the establishment of an Islamic state.

Yet, the currency of this clarion call conceals several anomalies. First, the Qur'an makes no mention of the Islamic state. This is not to say, though, that general principles that might underpin some conception of Islamic governance cannot be found in the Qur'an (or, for that matter, in the Sunna, or prophetic sayings, and Hadith, or accretion of accounts of these prophetic sayings). Rather, the point is that the Qur'an itself does not explicitly conceptualize the Islamic state. Hence, insofar as adherence to the teachings of Islamic scripture is a paramount demonstration of faith, any notion that their religion obliges Muslims to live in such a state is, at best, oblique. Second, scholars of Islamic studies have debated whether there has in fact ever been an "authentic" Islamic state in history, in the manner that Islamists in our contemporary era advocate. Prima facie, there appear many candidates for the mantle of a simulacrum – the Rashidun Caliphate (the first Islamic empire, formed right after the death of the Prophet Mohammad), the Mughal state, the Ottoman Empire, postrevolution Iran, modern Saudi Arabia, perhaps (setting aside its brutal and distasteful character) even ISIS. Nevertheless, their respective claims to authenticity have always been something of a bone of contention in one way or another. The larger point is that this dispute suggests ambiguity inherent in the concept, which has been open to interpretation. That the concept of an Islamic state derives from the time of the Prophet Mohammad's migration to Medina circa AD 622, where he established a community and functioned as its "prophet, law giver, chief judge, commander of the armies and civil head of State," with no established constitution, suggests why the term Islamic state is variously employed or (mis)understood in the contemporary period (Hitti 1949: 139). Indeed, it is precisely this ambiguity that explains the diverse "models" that have emerged to claim the mantle of authenticity, whereas the reality is that there remains no consensus on what truly represents a bona fide Islamic political system (Mohammad Ayoob 2007).

Extensive debates arise even within the community of Islamists over the question of how an Islamic state comes about. Some have argued for its imposition through a top-down approach, while others prefer a bottom-up process that begins with the Islamization of society at a grassroots level, creating Muslims who become more pious and religious, for whom the desire to champion the formation of an Islamic state would then follow as a natural, and inevitable, extension if not culmination of this religiosity. Some have even suggested that Islamists have managed to transcend the exclusivism often associated with the ideology, in order to embrace a "post-Islamist" turn that manifests in a more pluralistic, inclusive, and accommodative approach to the assertion of Islamic identity (Bayat 2007). Debates also revolve around the means through which to bring an Islamic state into being. Some advocate for peaceful activism within prevailing constitutional frameworks, including participation in elections, while others support more active resistance. At one end of this spectrum, some have contended that whether or not a moderate Islamist agenda gains traction depends on the ability of Islamists to evolve a discourse that can successfully explain and justify pluralist ideas in Islamic terms (Schwedler 2009). At the other, we have seen Islamists resort to militancy and even terrorism to achieve their ends. Moreover, we can further distinguish between those using militant means within the parameters of the nation-state and those who agitate to transcend national boundaries through a transnational jihad, the latter sometimes entertaining apocalyptic narratives in their ideologies as well.

In tandem with the concept of an Islamic state, another key idea and signifier of Islamist discourse is the *shari'a*, the body of canonical law associated with the Qur'an and the traditions of the Prophet – or more accurately, the introduction of *shari'a* into politics. Simply put, the stock-in-trade of Islamist social and political activism is the drive to elevate *shari'a* as the governing law of the land. Doing so reinforces Islam's essence as a religion of law and jurisprudence, given that *shari'a* in orthodox Islamic thought derives not only from the Qur'an, the Sunna, and Hadith, but also from the legal opinions, or fatwa, of Islamic scholars.

Finally, embedded in Islamism is the belief that political authority should reside in the hands of religiopolitical leadership, such that religious leaders would assume an explicit and central role. In Islamic history, this belief has found expression in the office of caliph. Curiously, the notion of clerical rule – not to be confused with the definitively political office of caliph – was born of the Shi'a tradition of governance as articulated by the religious leadership following the Iranian Revolution of 1979, when they introduced the Vilayat-i-faqih.[5] In quintessentially Sunni Malaysia, however, Islamists in PAS have replicated this model. In Indonesia during the 1950s, Islamists from both Masyumi and the Nahdlatul Ulama (NU) attempted to impose a requirement that upper-house legislatures be populated, if not dominated, by clerics vested with veto powers. A further anomaly is worth noting: Whereas religiopolitical leadership appears instrumental to the Islamist agenda, the driving force behind Islamism itself has often been the Muslim middle-class intelligentsia more than the religious establishment (Halpern 1963). Concomitantly, this is also perhaps why neither the source nor exercise of authority is confined to established religious institutions or hierarchies. As Richard Nielsen rightly observes:

> Many treatments of Islamic authority focus on "the authorities" – those individuals who hold official positions in governments and religious organizations – while overlooking those who do not have an appointment in some religious or political hierarchy. But this emphasis mistakes institutional

---

[5] Vilayat-i-faqih refers to a political system rooted in Shi'a tradition that is predicated on the guardianship and leadership of supreme clerics. The foremost examples, Ruhollah Khomeini and Ali Khamenei of Iran and Hassan Hasrallah of Hezbollah in Lebanon, are Shi'a clerics.

position in a hierarchy for actual influence. In fact, "the authorities" in Islam do not necessarily exercise any genuine authority. (Nielsen 2016: 3)

This is a pertinent point in the context of social movements, as they tend not to adhere to strict hierarchies.

2.2 Mobilizing Structures

As the previous section makes clear, ideas and ideals are important to mobilization in how they give meaning and purpose to action. But to be effective, they still need to be put into action. Whether for social movements or political parties, mobilizing structures, in terms of organizational capabilities and networks that provide the vehicles through which individuals act collectively to bring about political outcomes, are crucial. Importantly, structure, in this sense, is not antithetical to agency but rather facilitates it. Successful mobilization depends heavily on the organizational structures and capabilities a movement possesses and the networks into which they are integrated, for these are "key transmission belts of collective identity, drawing the ideas, sensibilities, [and] reflexivity of people together while criss-crossing social, economic, and political hierarchies" (Singerman 2004: 144). Correspondingly, the work of Santiago Anria highlights the importance of organizational structures and capabilities as well as networks in the context of Islamist activism to how Islamic social movements that emerged in Malaysia and Indonesia gradually evolved their political nature and character through their engagement of political issues, amalgamation with mainstream political parties, and participation in politics (Anria 2019).

The organizational structures and capabilities social movements require to facilitate collective action have already been the subject of extensive inquiry in the field of social movement studies, especially in literature that concentrates on questions of organizational politics and decision-making (Rupp and Taylor 1987; Whittier 1995). The inquiry that follows does not intend to take a "deep dive" into the various Islamic social movements, or political parties for that matter, that are active in Indonesia and Malaysia per se, for doing so would require far more extensive treatment than is possible here. Rather, this study focuses on organizational capabilities of social movements and political parties in terms of structures and modalities created to embed and propagate ideas, the networks that bind them, and the points of convergence and divergence that define them. Comparison demonstrates that stronger networks enhance organizational capabilities, allowing more effective mobilization. For example, scholars have determined that political parties that are built on social movements retain a strong grassroots element that proffers advantages when it comes to mobilization and activism (Kitschelt 2006).

Social movement scholars define networks as "sets of nodes, linked by some form of relationship, and delimited by some specific criteria" (Diani 2003: 2). Networks can link individual movement actors with each other, individuals with organizations, and/or segments within organizations. Likewise, networks can assume a direct or indirect nature, in the sense that

> direct ties are present when two nodes are directly linked in explicit inter-action and interdependence, for example, two activists who know each other personally, or two organizations that jointly promote a rally. Indirect ties are assumed to exist between two nodes when they share some relevant trait or orientation – for example, interest in certain issues or in the same campaigns – yet without any face-to-face interaction. (Diani 2013: 835)

Operationally, networks function to achieve several ends. They facilitate recruitment, expand the pool of collective resources and scope of mobilization (beyond the movement), and enhance the prospects for cooperation among movements. Furthermore, they also facilitate deeper institutionalization, par-ticularly as movements evolve into political parties, as we shall see in the following sections. Such cooperation can assume either a more instrumentalist logic, where interests converge, or could be more substantive, where shared identities connect these actors and organizations, thereby laying the ground-work for more strategic and long-term cooperation and perhaps even merger. Networks have always been an integral element of social movement activism, given their ability to augment organizational capabilities to enhance the power and amplify the influence of movement actors. Networks may also address power differentials and level the playing field, Charles Tilly explains, by sustaining "series of interactions between power holders and persons success-fully claiming to speak on behalf of a constituency lacking formal representa-tion, in the course of which those persons make publicly visible demands for changes in the distribution or exercise of power, and back those demands with public demonstrations of support" (Tilly 1984: 306).

Networks and organizational capabilities play a crucial role in how Islamists mobilize, and how effective their modes, mechanisms, and modalities of mobil-ization prove to be, which in turn can shape larger trends of Islamism within Muslim societies. Indeed, Olivier Roy has stressed this point, arguing that some Middle Eastern governments' adoption and acceleration of conservative Islamist policies in the 1980s can be attributed to the growing popularity of nonstate Islamist movements (Roy 1998). Conceptually, studying Islamist networks and their organizational capabilities is especially important to under-standing how and why social movements institutionalize, integrate with, or morph into political parties, and the effects on party and movement once such integration and institutionalization occur. Grasping these processes sheds light on how crucial networks are to the organizational capabilities of both social movements and political parties in Muslim societies.

Islamist political parties either grow out of Islamic social movements or cooperate with them to advance their objectives in three ways. First, the most obvious and direct manner through which this transpires is the process of institutionalization, whereby social movements actually transform into political parties. This pattern is closely identified with the Ikhwanul Muslimin, the Muslim Brotherhood movement that morphed into political parties and contested elections in Egypt, Jordan, and Palestine (Gaza). In Indonesia and Malaysia, the Ikhwan influence is pronounced in PKS and PAS respectively, but also in the social movements from which they draw much of their membership. Indeed, PKS has come to see itself as a chapter of the Ikhwan, which has also acknowledged this relationship (Khalil Al-Anani 2016). Second, where elections are held, movements are able to articulate and pursue an electoral strategy. The Ikhwanul Muslimin parties have followed this path, too, but so have other movements, such as Jamaat-i-Islami and Jamaat Ulema Islam in Pakistan, Jammat-i-Islami Hind in India, and Jamaat-i-Islami in Bangladesh. Finally, the amalgamation of movement and party allows for optimum mobilization towards shared goals by virtue of access to networks, organizational structures, and resources.

In discussing networks and organizational capacities, we should also consider the role and application of communications technology, especially how they facilitate the building of loosely linked networks that are minimally dependent on central coordination or leadership, create new arenas of contention and collaboration (i.e. cyberspace), and allow the mustering of resources for collective action (Earl and Kimport 2011). In the present social milieu, these new trends cannot be overemphasized. As Bennet describes:

> The innovative design and diffusion of communication and information technologies increasingly embeds those technologies in face-to-face experiences such as organizing, meeting, talking with friends, scheduling future protests, remembering and learning from past events, coordinating local protest actions in real time as they happen, and reporting them back through digital media channels so they can be recognized by activists themselves, as part of larger-scale developments. (Bennet 2005: 206)

The Muslim world has encountered these new trends in communication and information diffusion in a definitive manner. The advent of technologies such as the smartphone and other mobile Internet devices has allowed access to information on a scope and scale never before available for the general population.

Cultural and religious entrepreneurs have seized upon this state of affairs through the production of Islamic educational material and commentaries in the form of blogs, online journals, and other alternative media platforms to propagate ideas on religion and its role in society. In so doing, prevailing parameters of Islamic discourse have been challenged, if not undermined, while identities and consciousness are reconceptualized as a result of this explosion of information articulated by new voices (Anderson 2000: 39).

At the same time however, it is imperative to also recognize that

> how people use technologies, through effectively or poorly leveraging a technology's affordances, makes a difference to social processes. Technologies don't change societies or social processes through their mere existence but rather impact social processes through their mundane or innovative uses, and the ways in which the affordances of the technology are leveraged by those mundane or innovative uses. Another way of saying this is that it is people's usage of technology – not technology itself – that can change social processes. (Earl and Kimport 2011: 14)

In fact, the emergence of new media platforms in the information landscape can be – and has been – used to amplify and accelerate efforts at recruitment and mobilization in the case of the Tarbiyah and Dakwah movements.

2.3 The Context for Mobilization and Collective Action

Social movement theorists have identified political opportunity structures as a critical conceptual dimension in the study of collective action and mobilization. Broadly speaking, political opportunities can be defined as "consistent but not necessarily formal, permanent, or national signals to social or political actors which either encourage or discourage them to use their internal resources to form social movements" (Tarrow 1996: 54). Offering another perspective, Ruud Koopmans avers that opportunities are "options for collective action, with chances and risks attached to them, which depend on factors outside the mobilizing group" (Koopmans 2004: 65). In essence, both views refer to the same thing: the contextual structures that may encourage collective actors to form or join social movements to advance an agenda and determine whether mobilization would be more or less successful.

The case has already been made for the influence of Islam in politics and public life in many Muslim societies. The role that faith assumes in framing outlooks and shaping responses to developments around Muslims has, in many respects, gained speed. Indeed, for not a few adherents to the Islamic faith, the modernist idea that religion should be confined to the realm of private space and cannot conceivably take precedence over other motivations is not only untenable and unfathomable but, to their minds, fundamentally at odds with the principles of their faith as they see it (Liow 2016). In keeping with this view, not surprisingly, many Muslims see little distinction between their faith and their politics, understood in terms of electoral, legal, and institutional forms of engagement. The late L. Carl Brown averred that Islam in fact prescribes a certain form of politics in which the *din* (religion) is not separate from the *dawla* (state), and Muslims have an obligation to the affairs of the *dunya* (world) as they aspire to achieve the "divinely ordained political community in this world" (Brown 2000: 1). According to this framework, the three *d*s of *din*, *dawla*, and *dunya*, "cohered to provide a distinctly Islamic approach to political life" (Brown 2000: 1).

At the same time, efforts to suppress Islamic political engagement – whether overt or covert – have fared poorly at eroding the popular appeal of Islamism (Kuru 2019). Evidence from a range of cases, including Egypt, Algeria, Pakistan, and Jordan, suggests such efforts have mostly served to reinforce the Islamist narrative of resistance to oppression as a demonstration of piety; to drive Islamist organizations underground for a time, after which they have subsequently reemerged to pose an equally, if not more, robust challenge to the status quo; and even to spark Islamist violence targeting not only the state but also its citizenry. As alluded to in the preceding section, existing scholarship on Islamism in the Middle East and North Africa offers abundant evidence that the oppression of Islamist groups, whether political parties or social movements, has in fact strengthened, not weakened, Islamism (Claessen 2010; Wickham 2013; Mandaville 2014; Mecham and Chernov-Hwang 2014; Shadi Hamid and McCants 2017). In Europe, too, pressure to assimilate sharpens tension between Muslim and non-Muslim communities with competing views on religious identity and practice.

To be sure, similar tension has also manifested in Southeast Asia, but it is tempered by different demographics. Simply put, while Muslim minorities in Southeast Asia, such as in the southern provinces of Thailand and the southern islands of the Philippines, experience alienation and resentment not unlike that of their coreligionists in Europe (with the important distinction that many Southeast Asian Muslim minorities are considered indigenous, whereas those in Europe are, for the most part, immigrant communities), in Southeast Asian Muslim-majority states, it may be those majorities who impose religiously defined norms, values, and outlooks upon public and political life. In fact, even within Muslim-majority states in Southeast Asia, Muslim minority subgroups and sects have also experienced similar alienation. In this respect, Muslim alienation manifests in two ways in Southeast Asia that mirror the context confronting Christians, Jews, Yazidis, and in some cases, followers of smaller Muslim sects in the Middle East, who encounter discrimination and marginalization: among Muslims who constitute a demographic minority in a state where the majority population is non-Muslim, and among Muslim minority subgroups and sects who find themselves persecuted in a Muslim-majority, namely orthodox Sunni, setting.

Even then, the case can be made that the plight of non-Muslim minorities in the Middle East may sometimes have less to do with policies of Islamist governments than those of autocratic secular-nationalist regimes, for whom targeting non-Muslim minorities serves as a convenient means to shore up their religious credentials with minimal risk and cost, insofar as the larger Muslim-majority population is concerned.

That last observation speaks to another important issue: Notwithstanding the celebrated universal character of Islam, exemplified in the institutions of the *Haj* pilgrimage and the concept of the *Ummah*, or universal brotherhood of believers, the reality is that Islam is hardly monolithic in terms of subscription to a uniform body of beliefs. On the contrary, there is – and always has been – a rich diversity of thought and practice that comprise what is today the fastest-growing religion in the world. Indeed, this diversity also manifests in how widely varied Islamic social movements are in their vision, activities, and organizational structure. At times, this diversity has given rise to conflicts within Muslim communities, such as between groups that seek to achieve objectives via peaceful or militant means, or even between majoritarian impulses of orthodox Islamic schools of thought and the existential anxieties of minority sects. In fact, it can be argued that these intrareligious tensions can sometimes pose obstacles to the success of the Islamist agenda.

Among the most frequent explanations for the rise of Islamism is the argument that in the Middle East and North Africa, as well as Turkey, issues ranging from corruption and mismanagement to alternative priorities and simple incompetence have prevented many states from providing much needed welfare and social-security infrastructure to alleviate the material suffering of large segments of their population (Bayat 2002; Öniş 2006; Walsh 2006; Cammett and Luong 2014). Islamist groups have stepped into the void and assumed the role of quasi states, providing critical services such as education, healthcare, and employment for the disenfranchised. At the same time, these states' failure to deliver catalyzed agitation for a more capable/competent alternative model of government and governance. This gave rise to the clarion call for an Islamic state, the hallmark of all card-carrying Islamists. Of course, the question arises whether those who support Islamist groups do so because of the (religious) ideas and ideologies these groups propagate as their program for reform, or because of the material help they provide. Arguably, this ambiguity could account for both the opportunities and constraints that concurrently confront Islamists. Another version of this argument posits that the combination of disenfranchised youths and a growing middle class amid the climate of nationalism and anticolonialism that marked the two decades after the Second World War created a fertile environment for Islamism to flourish (Kepel 2002).

These propositions fit awkwardly with Islamists in Southeast Asia, whose encounters with politics have been different from those of their co-religionists elsewhere. In Indonesia, there was certainly repression, especially during the authoritarian New Order regime of President Suharto, which effectively circumscribed a previously dynamic terrain of Islamic political activism. Mainstream Islamists in Malaysia, however, have never had to deal with that level of repression, although they have been confronted by all the disadvantages that bedevil opposition political actors in a semiauthoritarian electoral democracy. The point is that Muslims in neither Indonesia nor Malaysia have had to contend with either marginalization as an ethnic or religious community or the social and economic disadvantages that have plagued their coreligionists in Muslim-majority countries in the Middle East and North Africa. On the contrary, from the 1970s to the 1990s, the Indonesian and Malaysian economies were among the fastest growing in the world.

2.4 Islam as Social Action

Notwithstanding the premise of engagement in politics as central to the definition of Islamism, Islamist movements do tap into a deeper reservoir of social movement activism. Indeed it would be simplistic to dismiss Islamism as merely "an ideology of protest," or to view its discourse, as some scholars do, as "rigid and simplistic, and rarely worked out beyond the level of slogan chanting" (Woltering 2002: 1134). There are three reasons why any effort to understand Islamism and the prospects of political power for Islamist groups in Southeast Asia must consider Islamist civil society activism and mobilization.

First, most scholars and observers agree that there has been an overall upsurge in religious piety and consciousness among Southeast Asian Muslims at large. While much of this increase in piety has been expressed in personal choices – Muslims are more diligent in observing the five pillars of the faith, are dressing more conservatively, and have taken to using Arabic forms of greeting rather than local languages – it has also manifested itself in greater social and cultural activism. Noorhaidi Hasan, in his earliest observations of the Salafi movement in Indonesia, noted that its expansion was "made evident in the appearance of young men wearing long beards (*lihya*), Arab-style flowing robes (*jalabiyya*), turbans (*imama*), and trousers right to their ankles (*isbal*) and women wearing a form of enveloping black veil (*niqab*) in public places" (Noorhaidi Hasan 2007: 83). Concomitantly, Muslims in Southeast Asia joined Islamic civil society organizations in droves, particularly welfare and educational bodies. This shift in the register of personal piety is also strongly evident in the growing popularity of Islamic education across Southeast Asia. Again, the crux of the matter is not so much that every Muslim is, ipso facto, an Islamist of sorts, but rather, that this upsurge in awareness and consciousness lends itself to politicization at the hands of political entrepreneurs.

Second, given an upsurge of social activism, we can hypothesize that political engagement will follow, to at least some degree. At a theoretical level, this speaks to ongoing debates about the distinction between cultural and political movements, and whether the former are inherently apolitical (Buechler 1995: 447). The reality, as we shall see, is that a considerable number of activists in social movements in Indonesia and Malaysia have joined Islamist political parties, with many of them rising to assume leadership positions. In essence, then, Islamic social and protest movements have themselves mobilized and either deepened their collaboration with or transformed into political parties, contesting elections in order to secure decision-making power. Indeed, some former social movement activists have successfully entered parliament or government via those channels.

Third, state sponsorship of Islamic activism has reached fairly high levels in recent years in Indonesia and Malaysia. This is evident, for instance, in the healthy allocation of resources to respective Islamic religious establishments. The Malaysian budget for 2019 set aside RM1.3 billion (USD300 million) for Jabatan Agama Kemajuan Islam Malaysia (JAKIM; Malaysian Islamic Development Department) and has been hovering around RM1 billion annually for the last few years, whereas the Indonesian ministry for religious affairs was funded to the tune of IDR2.9 trillion (USD177 million) in 2018, an increase from IDR0.9 trillion in 2014. Likewise, the staffing of such institutions has increased steadily over the years, testifying further to the growing role that the religious bureaucracy has come to play in both countries. What this suggests is that the state is prepared to invest resources to create an environment that generates greater religious consciousness. This environment can easily become one that facilitates Islamic activism, where political forces deploy instruments of the state to shore up their religious credentials through co-optation of Islamist activists and outcompeting the Islamist opposition by pushing and pulling the levers of state power to brandish their own religious credentials in a process that some scholars have termed "Islamization." Conversely, the state can regulate Islamist activism through the use of legal and bureaucratic mechanisms and has done so effectively in both Indonesia and Malaysia, even as civil society groups leverage opportunities created by the state for purposes of mobilization (Wiktorowicz 2000).

3 The Signifiers of Islamist Activism

Religious ideas from the Islamic heartland and South Asia have been arriving on Southeast Asian shores to influence and shape indigenous understandings and practices of Islam since the region's first encounters with the religion as early as the eleventh century. However, in the nineteenth century, this process gathered momentum with the arrival of the steamship, which allowed large numbers of Southeast Asian Muslims to travel to the Arabian peninsula for pilgrimages and study. During these sojourns, many of them came into contact with new political precepts and ideas, experienced the social and political environments that spawned them, and built relationships and incipient networks. In many respects, this process continues today.

Advances in transportation such as the advent of the steamship facilitated easier access to the Islamic heartland and its great centers of faith and learning, such as the Masjid al-Haram in Saudi Arabia, Al-Azhar University in Egypt, and Aligarh in India, exposing Southeast Asian Muslims to developments not only in Islamic religious thought but increasingly, social and political activism. This was particularly so in the late nineteenth and early twentieth centuries, when a potent mix of Islamic reformism and anticolonialism emerged in Cairo through the vehicle of scholarship produced by notable reformist thinkers such as Muhammad Abduh and, later, Rashid Rida. Inspired by their ideas, sojourning Southeast Asian Muslims became the conduit for the diffusion of Islamic reformism back to Southeast Asia, through the proliferation of modernist Islamic schools, the germination of publishing houses that translated these ideas into the local lingua franca, and the creation of various Muslim social movements that sought to engage the issues of the day through Islamic lenses, including anticolonialism and nationalism. Through these movements, issues of Islamic identity became deeply entwined with nationalism in British Malaya and the Dutch East Indies during the pre–World War Two years and remained so until independence.

Echoing the climate of the early twentieth century, the late 1960s and early 1970s ushered in another era of revival and reform, catalyzed by events and challenges that beset the Islamic world (Esposito et al. 1991; Lapidus 1997; Kepel 2002). In the main, the Islamic revival of this period has been attributed to the failure of pan-Arabism and Arab nationalism in the wake of military defeat by Israel. This led to the emergence (some would say resurgence) of Islamic reform movements across the Middle East that sought to reconceptualize the role of religion in Muslim societies, with an emphasis on returning to the fundamentals of Islam in terms of the understanding and practice of the faith. Needless to say, the impact of these crises extended beyond the Arab states and would precipitate reform across the Muslim world, including among coreligionists in Southeast Asia.

In Southeast Asia, the primary conduits of this Islamic revivalist discourse were Indonesian and Malaysian students who had traveled on scholarships to the storied Islamic centers of learning in both the Middle East and North Africa (Egypt in particular), and also, curiously enough, to Europe. Muslim student and welfare associations there, such as the Federation of Student Islamic Societies in the UK, which was popular among the large number of Malaysians studying, for instance, medicine at St. Andrews and Edinburgh, very quickly became the intellectual vanguard for Islamic reform. Upon their return to Southeast Asia, though obviously not the only conduits of such influence, these students seeded Islamic social movements designed to propagate the ideas and ideals of Islamic reform that had earlier shaped their own thinking on developments in their home countries. In Indonesia and Malaysia, this effort was best epitomized in the Tarbiyah and Dakwah movements respectively. In the Arab-Islamic lexicon, *tarbiyah* refers to education, whereas *dakwah* (or *da'wah*) means "a call to Islam," or proselytization. Etymology aside, at the heart of both movements was the objective of encouraging Muslims towards deeper faith and practice predicated on a better understanding of Islam (education) and preaching its universality (proselytization). In this way, it was envisaged to be a "bottom up" process whereby strengthening the personal piety of individual Muslims would translate into a collective effort to rebuild society in accordance with Islamic principles. While both terms refer to Islamic concepts relating to aspects of religious activity engaged in or conducted as expressions of piety, in the context of Indonesia and Malaysia, they also provide the nomenclature for broad Islamic socioreligious mass movements.

While there are broad similarities between the Tarbiyah and Dakwah movements in Indonesia and Malaysia, respectively, there were also discernible differences. For starters, while Tarbiyah was prevalent in both secular universities and Islamic education institutions in Indonesia, Dakwah in Malaysia was, for the most part, focused on the mobilization of graduates from secular tertiary institutions both in the country and abroad. The degree of political engagement also differed between Tarbiyah and Dakwah. At least in part because of the political climate (to be discussed at greater length in Section 4), the Tarbiyah movement was compelled by circumstance to be avowedly apolitical for a period, essentially because of the circumscription of political activities by the New Order Indonesian state between 1966 and 1998. To some degree, this explained its more nebulous character. On the other hand, while the Dakwah movement in Malaysia claimed to be, if not apolitical, then certainly "neutral," the reality was that its constituent movements, such as ABIM, engaged deeply in the politics of the day through protests, public speeches, discussion groups, and lobbying: in other words, with all the attributes of conventional social movement collective action.

3.1 Tarbiyah and Dakwah as Movements

In Indonesia, Islamic social and religious activism during the early years of the Suharto presidency revolved around DDII, formed in 1968 for purposes of formalizing the effort to awaken Islamic consciousness among Indonesian tertiary-education students through a focus on *dakwah* programs in university campuses and the organization of *dakwah* training (Ai Fatimah Nur Fuad 2017). Like their counterparts in Malaysia and, indeed, elsewhere in the Muslim world, the leaders of this movement were inspired and influenced by the Ikhwanul Muslimin. The writings of Sayyid Qutb, the Egyptian Ikhwan intellectual who was a staunch proponent of the argument that Muslims had to reject Western influences and revive Islam by reorganizing themselves in strict adherence to its original teachings – and significantly, that this process had to be catalyzed and led by a vanguard – have proved particularly popular.[6] Inspired by Qutb and others, DDII concluded that *dakwah* activism was, at its core, an intellectual exercise predicated on the need to counter *ghazwul fikri* or a "war of ideas," alluding to the ideological contest between the Muslim world and the West. This perspective translated to activism on a range of issues in response to developments in the Middle East, especially as they related to American support for Israel. In this vein, its adherents cast *dakwah* as a response (if not panacea) to the cultural imperialism of the West, but also as a means for Muslims to revive Islamic values and identities.

The chief vehicle of this Islamic activism was Tarbiyah. Explaining Tarbiyah in the Indonesian context, Salman described it as a "systematic method used to educate Muslims to understand Islam in the ideal manner so that they then have characteristics all Muslims should have like strong and clear beliefs, true practice of Islamic rituals, good ethics, economic independence, and a clean method of thinking" (Salman Salman 2006: 183). At its core, Tarbiyah was essentially about personal piety and religiosity; but for the movement, these traits were also to be related to the broader society (Febrian Taufik Saleh 2015). Articulated in this manner, the concept of Tarbiyah as expressed in the Indonesian context reflected its origins in Egypt, where Hassan al-Banna,

---

[6] The definitive statement of this remains Qutb's classic *Milestones*, which has been translated into Bahasa Indonesia and Malay. Of course, this is not to say that DDII was exclusively focused on Qutb's writings, or on Hassan al-Banna's for that matter. Their reading list was far more extensive. Having said that, in keeping with much of Ikhwan tradition, DDII saw the writings of these personalities to be seminal texts and hence used them extensively.

founder of the Ikhwanul Muslimin, appropriated it as an organizational basis for "spiritual enhancement [and] as [a] way to transfer Islamic knowledge and other skills ... cultivating theology (*tawhid*), moral issues (*akhlaq*), and thought (*fikrah*) ... among students who have become disillusioned with the politics of their times" (Hidayatullah 2000). This framing marked the inception of the extensive influence and impact that the Ikhwanul Muslimin would come to exercise on Islamic social and political movements in Indonesia.

Much in the same vein, Islamic social movement activism in postcolonial Malaysia was closely linked to the Islamic Dakwah movement that originated in the 1970s, around the same time that Tarbiyah was gaining purchase in Indonesia, with the emergence of a diverse set of student associations and other civil society organizations that sought to strengthen the religious identity of Malaysian Muslims. In a marked contrast with the Indonesian experience, however, they also mobilized by lobbying the Malaysian state to introduce Islamic values into its policy formulation and implementation processes. The Dakwah movement also differed from precursors such as the early nationalist movements and the growing popularity of PAS in the 1950s by dint of the profile of most of its followers. Whereas these earlier iterations of Islamic activism were propelled by *ulama* and teachers/graduates of Islamic studies from primarily rural backgrounds, the Dakwah movement that began in the 1970s was spearheaded by and involved urban-based middle-class professionals. As Zainah Anwar observed:

> In Malaysia, the young people make up the most active members of Islamic movements. They are high school and university students, graduates and young professionals who form the most receptive social group to the ideology of Islamic revivalism. Contrary to stereotypes, most Islamic revivalists are not uneducated, anti-modern, and society misfits, but are in fact well-educated, upwardly mobile and motivated individuals. In Malaysia, they form the backbone of Islamic revivalism. They range from highly qualified graduates in science and technology from British and American universities to graduates in Islamic theology and jurisprudence from al-Azhar. They come from diverse backgrounds, from upper- and middle-class urbanites to poor rural dwellers whose entrance into the country's universities brought them their first exposure to city life. (Zainah Anwar 1987: 2)

In other words, like Tarbiyah, Dakwah was, in essence, an urban phenomenon.

Moreover, Dakwah emerged at a point when the Malaysian state introduced its New Economic Policy, which, among other things, provided affirmative-action opportunities for Malay-Muslim students to obtain government scholarships, which in turn allowed them to pursue tertiary education both at home and abroad.[7] In Malaysia, universities such as Universiti Malaya, Universiti Kebangsaan Malaysia, and later the International Islamic University of Malaysia became cradles for *dakwah* activism and conveyor belts for Malay-Muslim graduates who would populate the public sector, giving both form and substance to the "Islamization" of the Malaysian bureaucracy. As for students who ventured abroad to the illustrious religious education institutions in the Islamic heartland of the Middle East and North Africa, or to universities in the United Kingdom in particular, it was in the course of these sojourns that domestic students came into closer contact with the revivalist ideas of prominent Muslim scholars such as Hassan Al-Banna and the Pakistani philosopher Abul A'la Maududi, which formed the substance of discussions in the ubiquitous Islamic study groups that proliferated in these campuses (Wickham 2013: 196). Having been exposed to these ideas and having developed their own thinking on how *dakwah* and political functionalism fused together in an Islamic movement, these students would eventually assume the roles of the intelligentsia of the Dakwah movement and would prove instrumental to the propagation of revivalist ideas in Malaysia.

Another point of convergence between Tarbiyah and Dakwah was the emphasis on personal conviction and conversion. Islamic reformism, the wellspring from which Tarbiyah and Dakwah drew, was primarily predicated on personal encounters with the faith through familiarization with and understanding of key doctrines, and individual responsibility for and commitment to its propagation. This was expressed in the importance of education and, eventually, a robust cadreization program as a vehicle for ideational change, and in *dakwah* as the personalized means of spreading these ideas.

A feature of the Dakwah movement that distinguished it from its Indonesian counterparts at the time was the nature and character of the movement, which, as we shall soon see, bears on the ideas it promulgated. Dakwah was distinguishable by its overt political nature: It aimed not only to inspire personal piety but to translate it into a political agenda. The Tarbiyah movement in Indonesia was careful not to openly confront the state for fear of retaliatory suppression, especially after the New Order government of President Suharto introduced the "Normalization of Campus Life" decree in April 1978, which prohibited political activism on campuses. In contrast, the Dakwah movement,

---

[7] The New Economic Policy was introduced in 1971 following intercommunal electoral violence in 1969. The Policy was designed to "reduce and eventually eradicate poverty, by raising income levels and increasing employment opportunities for all Malaysians, irrespective of race" and to accelerate "the process of restructuring Malaysian society to correct economic imbalance, so as to reduce and eventually eliminate the identification of race with economic function" (Crouch 1996: 24–25). In essence, it was an affirmative-action policy to proffer economic and educational advantages to the predominantly Muslim Malay community.

notwithstanding the proscription of political activities on Malaysian campuses through legislation such as the 1971 Universities and University Colleges Act, proactively critiqued the perceived failure of the Malaysian government to inculcate Islamic values and practices in affairs of the state. By this measure, any suggestion that the Dakwah movement is apolitical would be misplaced (Azmil Tayeb 2018: 204–206).

Of course, one can argue the case that the movement was apolitical in the sense that it was not a political party, nor did it originate as an initiative from a political party (or the state, for that matter). Not unlike Tarbiyah in Indonesia, the appeal Dakwah activism possessed had much to do with the fragile moorings of Malay-Muslim identity at the time, as it encountered challenges in the form of both global and domestic developments. These included the acceleration of Islamic revivalism globally, which amplified the sense that Malay-Muslim identity was in crisis, as well as the May 13 race riots that broke out in 1969 and the rapid urbanization of Malaysia and the sense of dislocation it wrought on predominantly rural Malay-Muslim communities. Through these events, the common theme emerged of Islam under siege, thereby requiring reformation in the form of a return to fundamentals for it to flourish again. By this token, as a religious revival movement, Dakwah was very much born in the cauldron of Malaysian (and global) politics and deeply engaged with the issues of the day.

Needless to say, Tarbiyah and Dakwah were hardly the only Islamic social movements active in Indonesia and Malaysia during the height of Islamic reformism. Indeed, there were others of diverse ideological and organizational stripes such as the NU and Muhammadiyah in Indonesia, or al-Arqam in Malaysia. Nevertheless, Tarbiyah and Dakwah were two of the most recognizable and consequential of such movements in terms of their long-term bearing on politics. Moreover, the ideas they promulgated provided a template for the activism of other groups and shaped the Islamist discourse that would develop in these societies.

3.2 Islamic State, Islamic Law, Islamic Life

Consonant with Islamist activism elsewhere, the leitmotif of the Islamic state and the aspiration to introduce *shari'a* as part of national legislation have been axioms that have seized Islamists in Indonesia and Malaysia. To be sure, this was already evident very early on in the modern histories of the two countries. Islamists were key actors – indeed, arguably even the original actors – in the script of anticolonialism that unfolded in both Indonesia and Malaysia at the turn of the twentieth century with the rise of nationalist movements on both sides of the Melaka Straits. Islamic conceptions of nationhood figured prominently in the emergence of nationalist consciousness and thought in Indonesia, and the mobilization of Muslims and their subscription to a discourse of defiance articulated along religious lines formed something of a paradigm for later independence struggles among Islamists who sought to create an Islamic polity from the ashes of the Second World War (Liow 2016: 177–178). In the meantime, Islamist groups also contributed to the emergence of national consciousness in the pre–World War Two years in Malaysia. There, Islamists were found in early nationalist movements such as the Kesatuan Melayu Muda (Young Malays Union), Majlis Agama Tertinggi Malaya (the Supreme Religious Council of Malaya), and Hizbul Muslimin (Muslim People's Party of Malaya) (Roff 1967). At the core of what these Islamist elements advocated and mobilized to achieve in both Indonesia and Malaysia was the idea that the postcolonial state should be organized, foremost, on the principles of Islamic law or *shari'a*.

In Indonesia, how Islamic social movements and political parties have narrated the Islamic state in the context of Indonesian politics has, in large part, been framed by long-standing debates over Pancasila, the official ideological foundation of the postcolonial Indonesian state. The doctrine comprises five principles: (1) belief in a supreme god, (2) humanitarianism, (3) unity of Indonesia, (4) consultative democracy, and (5) social justice. The origins of the concept can be traced to the emergence of nationalism during the anticolonial struggle of the pre–World War Two era, which witnessed a proliferation of diverse movements that nevertheless shared the similar objective of overthrowing Dutch colonial rule. In many ways, the range of nationalist movements reflected the ethnic and linguistic diversity of the Dutch East Indies archipelago, not to mention the divergent historical encounters that these different ethnic, cultural, and geographical groups experienced with Dutch colonialism (Kahin 1985). Regardless, a central objective of an embryonic "Indonesian" nationalism was to find common ground on which a national struggle could be mobilized (Kahin 1952). It was in that spirit that the new postcolonial government – or nationalist leaders – articulated the Pancasila as a centripetal concept to foster national unity.

For Islamists who were part of this wider landscape of anticolonialism, however, the establishment of an Islamic state was the *sine qua non* of their movement. In the context of debates over Pancasila, this found expression in efforts to employ *shari'a* as the reference point for postcolonial state building, where the intent was to imbue the nascent constitution with a decidedly Islamic flavor. To that end, Islamists introduced the "*shari'a* clause," which sought to require that the preamble of the constitution include the clause "with the obligation for the followers of Islam to practice *shari'a*," into the debate

(Liow 2016: 185). For reasons that have been extensively discussed elsewhere, the proposed clause, known has the Jakarta Charter, was not adopted. In the ensuing years, the struggle was continued through mutually exclusive military and political means in the form of the Darul Islam rebellion and the political efforts of the Masyumi party. Indeed, such was its traction among Islamists that the debate resurfaced again in 2001, and although defeated (again), it nonetheless still testified to the traction of the idea and its appeal to certain segments of the Indonesian Muslim community (Buehler 2008).

The debate over Pancasila persists in present-day contexts in part because of the doctrine's ambiguity, which allows for varying and divergent interpretations among Islamist groups that seek to appropriate the concept as part of their respective agendas. To be sure, Pancasila has found advocates among the more progressive Islamic social movements, who have been comfortable reconciling it with the Islamic principles they argue are necessary foundations for Indonesian society. Illustrative of this, Muhammadiyah, the second biggest Muslim organization in Indonesia, has declared that "Pancasila is not a religion, but its substance contains and is in line with Islamic values. Pancasila is God's mercy for an independent and advanced Indonesian nation" (Republika 2012).

Meanwhile NU, the largest Muslim organization in Indonesia (and possibly the world), has frequently and consistently reiterated its formal declaration of the relationship between Islam and Pancasila, which it codified in 1983. The Declaration articulates five points on the matter: (1) Pancasila as the basis and philosophy of the Republic of Indonesia is not a religion, cannot replace religion, and cannot be used to replace religion; (2) Sila Ketuhanan Yang Maha Esa, or belief in a supreme god, as the basis of the State of the Republic of Indonesia according to article 29 paragraph (1) of the 1945 Constitution, which animates other principles, reflects *tawhid* (oneness of God) according to the understanding of faith in Islam; (3) for NU, Islam is creed and *shari'a*, covering aspects of human relationships with God and each other; (4) the acceptance and practice of Pancasila is the embodiment of efforts of Indonesian Muslims to practice *shari'a*; and (5) as a consequence of the above, NU is obliged to present a correct understanding of Pancasila and its pure and consequent practice by all parties (NU Online 2020b).

Arguably the most striking case for how Pancasila, and in particular, its first principle regarding "Belief in a Supreme God," has purportedly been reconciled with Islam in the Indonesian context is bizarrely captured in the ostensible endorsement it received from Front Pembela Islam (FPI), the extremist Islamic vigilante group whose motto is "NKRI Bersyari'ah" or the formal application of Islamic law within the unitary Indonesian Republic. FPI acknowledged that "the first article of Pancasila has to be viewed as the most fundamental teaching of Islam, that is, the Tauhid (the oneness of Allah). . . . Therefore, this article serves as the basis for the implementation of the commands and laws of Allah as the one and only God" (Fahlesa Munabari 2017: 249). Needless to say, advancing this train of thought allowed FPI to aggressively promote "Shari'aization" without drawing the ire of the state.

Unlike Muhammadiyah or NU, the Tarbiyah movement was more equivocal on the matter of Pancasila, especially in response to the New Order regime's move to impose it as the "sole principle" (*asas tunggal*) of all Islamic movements. Along with several other organizations, the Tarbiyah movement mobilized its network of study circles to chip away at Pancasila's dominance as *asas tunggal*. Doing so reflected the movement's belief that the successful preservation of Islamic ideology and promotion of its cause required endurance over the *longue durée* (Muhammad Sa'id 2003). One of the concerns that Tarbiyah had with regards to the narrative of *asas tunggal* was its prejudice against their advocacy on other signature issues, particularly *shari'a* and the Islamic state objective, issues kept alive in the Muslim consciousness in Indonesia through the efforts of several religious organizations and Islamic social movements, including Tarbiyah. As Martin van Bruinessen observed in reference to Tarbiyah

> they are highly critical of the secular state and believe that only a state based on *shari'a* can be just. They are relatively closed groups and avoid contact with outsiders. They assert that Islam is a total way of life and demand that their members conform to Islamic norms in all aspects of life. They exercise strict control of their members and demand high standards of Islamic morality. (Chernov-Hwang 2009: 56)

The fact that the Tarbiyah movement was careful not to advocate too vocally or visibly for an Islamic state, as was the case, should not be taken to suggest any dilution of their support for it. Rather, the movement viewed a measured approach to the question of *shari'a* implementation toward the ultimate longer-term objective of the Islamic state as the best course of action on account of tactical constraints. As Anthony Bubalo and Greg Fealy explained, the leadership of the Tarbiyah movement arrived at this conclusion on grounds that "until Islamic law and principles were well understood by Muslims, a viable Islamic state would be difficult to establish. Nonetheless, an Islamic state was seen as the endpoint of the struggle" (Bubalo and Fealy 2005: 68). In addition to these tactical considerations, there were political ones as well. The Tarbiyah movement arose out of a climate of suppression of publicly active Islamic groups during the New Order era, including close surveillance of *dakwah* activities and public study groups. Doubtless, these encounters with authoritarianism shaped the movement's approach to advocacy. It was only during the Reformasi era of openness in the 1990s (examined in Section 5) that Tarbiyah principles would be brought into sharper relief, through Partai Keadilan or the Justice Party (PK), later reborn as Partai Keadilan Sejahtera (the Prosperous Justice Party, PKS). PK/PKS saw itself as "agent[s] of the country's integration into liberal political and economic spaces" and cast Tarbiyah principles of *shirka iqstisadiyya* (ensuring economic growth and fair distribution) and *fikra ijtimaiyya* (commitment to resolving social problems), drawn from the political thought of Hassan al-Banna, into a narrative of politics of service on which its campaign platforms were predicated (Noorhaidi Hasan 2009: 18).

While the Islamization agenda may have been associated with Tarbiyah and its political offshoots, it was in no way the sole preserve of these groups. Indeed, the downfall of the New Order regime ushered in an era of democratization that breathed new life to Islamic activism hitherto silenced by the previous regime and paved the way for an upsurge in sociopolitical mobilization. This effervescence of Islamic discourse and engagement revived widespread discussions regarding the place of *shari'a* in Indonesian society, as evident in the debates over the Jakarta Charter mentioned earlier. Explaining its continued relevance, Muhammad Siddik of DDII explained:

> Syariah (*shari'a*) is often rejected. Indeed, there is no order to establish an Islamic state. However, the implementation of Syariah still requires effort. . . . Thus, Muslims have an obligation to implement Syariah in their personal lives, as well as in society. They should also uphold Syariah, and carry out the teachings in the Quran. . . . Islamic law is one of the materials that was agreed upon in the formation of Negara Kesatuan Republik indonesia (NKRI). (Republika 2019)

Much in the same vein, NU took the view that while it rejected the establishment of a caliphate, it was not opposed to the application of Islamic law in Indonesia. As Abdullah Syamsul Arifin, chairman of the Jember chapter of NU, maintained, "NU has never rejected Islamic law. In fact, NU was the first organization that brought Islam into the Nusantara, through the arts, culture, and customs. We brought in peaceful Islam. Therefore, if a group accuses NU of rejecting *syariah*, it means that it lacks historical understanding" (Times Indonesia 2017). Elsewhere, NU chairman H. Robikin Emhas explained that, in fulfillment of the national and religious mandates that the movement was committed to, "Indonesia is a peaceful country, one that is aligned with Islamic law" (NU Online 2020). Historically, NU has viewed nationalism and patriotism as extensions and expressions of religious obligation, thereby explaining the intertwined nature of the interest of the nation with the interest of the movement that is evident from its narrative (Faisal Ismail 2011: 278).

In Malaysia, Dakwah groups have been at the forefront, calling not only for Muslims to demonstrate piety at an individual level, but also for the introduction of stronger Islamic values to the norms and institutions that govern Malaysian society more broadly. This sentiment was captured in the motto of the standard bearer of the Dakwah movement, ABIM: "toward building a society that is based on the principles of Islam." Indeed, Dakwah groups have been instrumental in shaping emergent Islamist discourse, a central feature of which has been an intellectual, fundamentalist, and Arabic orientation. This has been a consequence of the movement's internalization of theological perspectives and concepts through their exposure to and training in the ideas originating from the Islamic resurgence in the Middle East by dint of the fact that, as suggested earlier, many Malaysian Muslim students either studied in Middle Eastern countries or, if they were educated locally, studied under graduates from these countries. In fact, as observed earlier, even those Malaysian Muslim students who went to the UK, Australia, and the USA for their tertiary education became exposed to these ideas through their participation in Islamic study groups and Muslim students' associations, where they interacted with coreligionists from these countries. In any event, these encounters set them at odds with the syncretic nature of traditionalist Islam of rural Malaysia, which still obtained during the 1970s as this Islamic resurgence gathered pace but was gradually being eroded in the face of rapid urbanization.

As an intelligentsia-based urban phenomenon in cosmopolitan Malaysia, ABIM has approached advocacy via the universalist principles of Islam. This has been significant in the context of Malaysia, where political rhetoric and narratives are persistently colored by conceptions of race, religion, and ethnicity, often in exclusivist and exclusionary terms. Much of the thinking in ABIM has been shaped by Islamic scholars and intellectuals associated with the movement. A case in point is the work of Mohd Kamal Hassan, a leading Malaysian scholar of Islam and an ABIM intellectual, who had expounded on concepts such as *aqalliyyat* (Islamic jurisprudence towards minorities), *al-hiwar al-hadari* (civilizational dialogue), and *al-mujtama al-madani* (civil society) in his extensive résumé of speeches and articles that have informed ABIM positions in relation to expressions of Islamic identity against the backdrop of cultural and religious pluralism in Malaysia (Mohd Kamal Hassan 1997). Underlying these concepts is the notion that the religious convictions of Muslims in Malaysia need not set them at odds with their non-Muslim neighbors. Given the upsurge of the ethnonationalist narrative of Malay-Muslim primacy beginning in the 1970s, the fact that ABIM sought to strike a conciliatory tone was notable, even if more polarizing political forces drowned out its narrative.

At the same time, even as its members engaged in public discussions, ABIM was also aware that its traditional emphasis on philosophical discourse had to eventually find expression in concrete actions. This was reflected in then-President Siddik Fadil's call for ABIM to look beyond discussions on philosophical frameworks to implement its teachings in Malay-Muslim society by adjusting to the realities and needs of the local culture (Siddik Fadil 1989: 44–66). It is interesting to note, however, that he expressed this desire for a more "applied" approach in response to the exodus of party members, triggered by the departure of its most iconic leader, Anwar Ibrahim, to launch his political career by joining the United Malays National Organization (UMNO) in 1982 (Mohd Anuar Tahir 1993: 4–5).

The Islamization program ABIM propagated was, like Tarbiyah's in Indonesia, very much predicated on education. Nevertheless, there was a notable difference. In Indonesia, the proliferation of Tarbiyah education programs occurred away from the scrutiny of the New Order state. In Malaysia, however, the government gave Dakwah organizations such as ABIM a wide remit to influence education policy at the national level. Needless to say, they seized upon these opportunities to introduce elements of religiomoralistic instruction in line with their ideas and concepts of Islamic identity and society. Consider, for instance, the Education Memorandum that ABIM submitted to the Malaysian government through then-education minister Mahathir Mohamad in 1975. The proposal drew on the ideas of Syed Naquib al-Attas, another ABIM intellectual stalwart, proposing spiritual and moral education as key elements of human development (Osman Bakar 1993). In explaining the need for religious content in education, Anwar accented the role of education as "an on-going effort towards further developing the potential of individuals in a holistic and integrated manner, so as to produce individuals who are intellectually, spiritually, emotionally and physically balanced and harmonious, based on a firm belief and devotion to God" (Anwar Ibrahim 1989: 65).

As an Islamic social movement, ABIM has been intent on stressing not only the conceptual understanding of Islamic precepts but also their applicability in everyday life. ABIM has supported the relevance of *shari'a* – including its penal code – in Malaysian society, even as it remained ambivalent on the goal of the formation of an Islamic state. Previously, ABIM leaders had frequently criticized the UMNO-led Malaysian government for foregrounding Malay nationalism at the expense of Islam, arguing that bestowing upon Islam the status of official religion in Malaysia was a necessary but insufficient expression of the centrality that it should be accorded. Instead, ABIM advocated that

Malaysia should prioritize the exercise of Islamic law and, ipso facto, the country's essence as an Islamic state (Ahmad Lutfi Othman 1992: 109). ABIM has since continued to maintain cautious support for Islamic law. When former prime minister Mahathir Mohamad criticized efforts by PAS to table a parliamentary bill on *hudud* (the Islamic penal code) in 2014, ABIM responded with a measured defense of the motion. According to its president, Amidi Abdul Manan, Mahathir's retort risked conveying the mistaken impression that "Islamic punishment is unreasonable and cruel … [when] the beauty of Islamic laws lies in its trial, justification and management" (Astro Awani 2014). At the same time, ABIM, along with other Islamic Dakwah activist groups, has also been aware of the political baggage behind the call for implementation of *hudud* as advocated by PAS and UMNO. They have hence sought to distance themselves from politicized debates over the issue. As Hew Wai Weng observed in the wake of discussions over efforts by PAS to introduce the aforesaid *hudud* bill:

> Major mainstream urban-based Muslim organizations such the Malaysian IKRAM Association and ABIM have been distancing themselves from the amendments, and perceive the whole exercise to be a political strategy by PAS. Generally speaking, they may in principle be supportive of efforts to enhance the existing *shari'a* courts, but differ from the current PAS leadership on the methods being used. (Hew 2017)

It should be noted, however, that ABIM has been less vocal an advocate for Islamic law and the Islamic state in more recent times, as the movement has gravitated away from the radical political discourse that defined the era of Anwar Ibrahim's leadership, choosing instead to emphasize lower-key community engagement.

Whereas ABIM was focused on high-profile social and political activism such as public protests, especially in the first decade of its existence, other Dakwah groups were not given as much to public displays of political activism, choosing instead to exert their influence in less visible ways. One such group that would eventually grow into a consequential force was the IRC, formed in 1975 by Malaysian students based in Brighton, UK, who were followers of the teachings of the Pakistani cleric and philosopher Abu A'la Maududi and his Jamaat-I-Islami party (Hassan Omar 2017). Like ABIM, IRC drew its support from Muslim tertiary-education students who were mostly educated abroad. Resembling more the Tarbiyah model in Indonesia than ABIM though, the IRC centered its mobilization strategies on low-key study groups that operated beyond the gaze of the state. IRC also took a stronger line on the Islamic state than ABIM: Whereas ABIM concerned itself with non-Muslim reactions to

Islamization, IRC often criticized the Malaysian state as "un-Islamic" and sought the formation of a more "authentic" form of Islamic government. Likewise, while ABIM eschewed the exclusivist discourse of race and advocated for the universalism of Islam, IRC embraced racial discourse by adopting a hard dichotomy between Muslim and infidel, Islamist and apostate (Ahmad Fauzi Abdul Hamid 2009: 148). To the IRC, because Malays are the majority ethnic group in Malaysia and are practically all followers of Islam, political and administrative power must logically lie in the hands of Muslims; ergo, calls for Islamic government and Islamic governance in the form of swift implementation of Islamic law are not only justified but required, and, indeed, obligatory.

However, its inability to gain traction through more hard-line positions led the IRC to shift toward a more moderate approach to engagement that resulted in its transformation into Jemaah Islah Malaysia (JIM) in 1990. An ostensibly more conciliatory Islamic movement, JIM made efforts to blunt the hard edges that characterized its predecessor in order to widen its appeal. JIM finessed the position of the IRC on Islamic strictures by taking the view that their implementation would entail a prolonged process and require *islah* (reform) through *tadrij* (gradual stages). Like ABIM, JIM prescribed the gradual infusion of ideas of Islamic governance into Malaysian society through formal and informal education programs targeted at raising the awareness and consciousness of Muslims in Malaysia regarding Islamic principles and values. This would then lead to changes over time (*tadrij*) to the Federal Constitution, as amendments would bring the formulation, implementation, and enforcement of law naturally into alignment with *shari'a* (Saari Sungib 1995). This gradual approach would eventually find its way into the thinking of reform-minded Islamists that populated PAS and later the Amanah party that the reformist or progressive faction of PAS formed in 2015 after they found themselves increasingly sidelined within the Islamist opposition party.

Yet even as ABIM and JIM sought to downplay the narrative of Malay-Muslim dominance, other Islamic groups emerged to amplify it. These included Ikatan Muslimin Malaysia (ISMA; Muslim Solidarity Front of Malaysia), which was formed in 1997 and agitated for society to uphold Islamic principles and for *Ketuanan Melayu* (Lordship of the Malays) to serve as the foundation of Malaysian identity. It did so by unapologetically advancing a pro-Malay, pro-Islamic narrative that shaped the right-wing turn towards ethnonationalism that occurred in UMNO after the 2013 elections (Mohamed Nawab Mohamed Osman and Saleena Saleem 2016: 3).

Whether in the tensions inherent between ABIM and the IRC models of Islamic society and governance, or in the emergence of newer advocates for Malay-Muslim rights such as ISMA, these groups all essentially illustrated the fact that while the ideas propagated by the Dakwah movement spoke to matters of personal piety, a larger social and political intent lay behind that praxis. It was in light of this layering that A. B. Shamsul surmised "one consequence of the Dakwah movement's development was that Islam came to be highlighted as the pillar of Malay identity" (Shamsul 1997: 210).

4 Movements and Parties, Mobilization and Transformation

Having introduced some of the Islamist ideas and ideals that underpinned Muslim social movements in both Indonesia and Malaysia from the time of the Islamic resurgence of the late 1960s and early 1970s, we turn now to the question of how these signifiers translated into collective action in terms of their organizational expression and engagement with the politics of the day, includ-ing, in some cases, transformation from social movements to political parties. Put differently, as social movement theory would suggest, if ideas form the essence of Islamist social movement activism, it follows that organizational structure and capabilities are the instruments through which activists catalyze mobilization deriving from those very ideas. In order to conceptualize the process through which these signifiers came to assume currency, not only in the political discourse that was taking shape in these countries but also in the building of collective (Islamist) identity, we turn to the organizational structure and capabilities that Islamist social movements possess, and the networks in which they are integrated. It is important to note too that the study of organiza-tional structures and mobilizing processes requires an appreciation of mobiliza-tion as a function of dynamic interactions between ideas and repertoires of contention that are innovative and evolving (for instance, with the creative use of digital media) rather than predetermined and static (McAdam, Tarrow, and Tilly 2001: 41–50).

Studies on political Islam and Islamist mobilization that draw from Arab examples frequently conclude that, by and large, it is the authoritarian structure of power that prevails in these countries that drives opposition away from the public sphere into the private. This opposition often find themselves coalescing around the mosque, the one institution that, for the most part, authoritarian states dare not confront, at least not directly. Concomitantly, mosques become quasi-legitimate physical and discursive space through which political engage-ment occurs. But the script unfolded somewhat differently in Southeast Asia, notwithstanding some resonance, particularly in Indonesia during the more authoritarian years of the New Order regime. In Indonesia, while the visibility of mosques meant that they came under close scrutiny, it was through educa-tional institutions that Islamic social movements found greater latitude to operate, away from the probing eyes of the state. Given the diversity of streams of Islam in Indonesia, it should hardly be surprising that a wide canvas of educational institutions has emerged, each contributing in its own way to the process of mobilization and social transformation by providing leadership, resources, and networks through which they exercise considerable power and influence. Rooted in *dakwah*, the Tarbiyah movement is instructive in this regard. Because of restrictive policies the state enforced during the New Order era, many Muslim leaders and Islamist movements used ubiquitous *dakwah* programs as means to keep Islamic activism alive but, importantly, outside the parameters of mainstream politics. Programs such as *Bina Masjid Kampus* (Initiative to Build Campus Mosques) and *Latihan Mujahid Dakwah* or LMD (Training for Islamic Propagation Warriors) established by DDII provided the necessary platform for activism and set the stage for deeper engagement through the vehicle of Islamic education. To that end, as Yudi Latif observed, the "network of the *dakwah*-oriented young intellectuals with the DDII group provided the channel for the transmission of Islamic historical ideas and the impetus for the mosque movement that became more apparent from the early 1970s" (Yudi Latif 2008: 363).

One of the remarkable characteristics that scholars have noted about the Tarbiyah movement is its strong cadreization structure (Bubalo and Fealy 2005). This cadreization structure was established on the back of an extensive Islamic school network that had gradually expanded since the 1970s, and which served as the signal expression of the organizational and institutional reach and capacity of the Tarbiyah movement. By some accounts, the number of Islamic schools in Indonesia has ballooned to more than 100,000 of different doctrinal, ideological, and political persuasions.[8] According to Robert Hefner, since the fall of the New Order regime, a considerable number of these have been integrated Islamic schools (schools that weave religion through all subjects in their comprehensive curriculum), with many linked to the Tarbiyah movement (Hefner 2009: 74). Additionally, many of these institutions are privately funded by foreign benefactors, thereby introducing a transnational element to the mobilization that they facilitate (Suharto 2018). It is this channel that has given rise to fears of "Arabization" and the "infiltration" of ideas hitherto

---

[8] These include *pesantren* and *madrasah*. Data from the Data, Information System, and Public Relations Section of the Secretariat of the Directorate General of Islamic Education at the Ministry of Religion shows that in 2016 there were 28,194 *pesantrens* scattered both in urban and rural areas with 4,290,626 students (Republika 2017). Meanwhile, the latest data (2019/2020) from the office of the Secretariat Director-General of Islamic education under the Ministry of Religious Affairs counts 82,418 *madrasahs* across Indonesia (Kementerian Agama RI 2019/2020).

foreign to Indonesia's Muslim culture, although the reality is far more compli-
cated (Van Bruinessen 2018).

While the first evidence of Islamic student activism was already surfacing in
the late 1960s, it proliferated in the 1980s and 1990s, hastened by Indonesian
students returning primarily from Egypt. The ideas that were infused into and
percolated through Indonesian Muslim society have been discussed previously.
Suffice it to add that these Ikhwan-inspired Indonesian student leaders also
brought back with them ideas about organization and mobilization tactics
centered on the *usrah* (literally "family," referring to close-knit Islamic study
groups and circles) or, in Indonesian parlance, *liqo*. Hefner succinctly summar-
izes the organizational structure of Tarbiyah in the following manner:

> Brotherhood-inspired support groups of this sort typically consist of eight to
> sixteen same-sex individuals, under the guidance of a centrally appointed
> leader (*naqib*).[9] The *naqib* in turn receives guidance from a higher-ranking
> individual in the organization, with whom he alone has contact. Once estab-
> lished, these support groups are supposed to serve as the nucleus for commu-
> nities (*jemaah*) of pious Muslims. Their behavior is supposed to be so
> ethically exemplary that it gradually brings about the transformation of
> society and – through nonviolent means and at some unspecified future
> date – the state. (Hefner 2009: 75)

With this structure, the Tarbiyah movement would gradually expand its influence during this period, particularly among state-controlled religious institutions, capturing student leadership bodies in various state Islamic universities
along the way. This provided the movement a beachhead from which it would
deepen its political engagement when the political tide began to turn in the late
1990s. Of course, it is important to register that those institutions associated
with the Tarbiyah movement are not the only ones that have invested in
mobilization. Indeed, a broad range of schools and institutions linked to
Muhammadiyah, NU, Hidayatullah, and several other, smaller movements, all
with their own networks and structures, have also served as vehicles for
mobilization.

In Malaysia, the reach of the Dakwah movement in the realm of education
was facilitated by networks of private Islamic schools associated with groups
such as ABIM, JIM, and Pertubuhan Ikram Malaysia, as well as PAS. In the case
of ABIM, its outreach and mobilization efforts in the earlier years of its
existence were concentrated on tertiary institutions, where its influence over
student associations and establishment of *usrah* study groups served to expand
its presence. Of course, government policies that privileged Malay-Muslims for

---

[9] Another commonly used term for cell leader in Indonesia is *murobbi* or *murabbi*.

entry into these institutions further facilitated these efforts; tertiary institutions fast became fertile ground for Dakwah recruitment and activism. As alluded to heretofore, the New Economic Policy introduced in 1971 provided opportunities by way of quotas for Malay-Muslim students, many from rural segments of Malaysian society, in fields such engineering and the natural and physical sciences, fields in which non-Malays traditionally excelled. The difficulties of adjusting to urban life and tertiary studies precipitated an upsurge in piety among Malay-Muslim students, many of whom had turned to Islam for respite. Their needs were met by *usrah* organized by ABIM and other Dakwah-affiliated study groups that mushroomed in campuses across the country, so much so that, as Ahmad Fauzi Abdul Hamid describes, "to all intents and purposes, to ABIM, the *usrah* had supplanted the madrasah as the cardinal educational and social institution for Malay-Muslims. The multi-dimensional *tarbiyah* syllabus intended to create not spiritual recluses, war guerillas or one-track minded individuals, but rather missionary characters [who] harmoniously integrated their respective purity, courage, and academic brilliance" (Ahmad Fauzi Abdul Hamid 2003: 65).

While Malaysian Dakwah groups actively recruited and mobilized through tertiary institutions, they also built schools at the kindergarten, primary, and secondary school levels that served, in a sense, as feeder institutions. In the case of ABIM, these schools have been managed by (graduate) members and use textbooks produced by ABIM. Of note is the fact that, not unlike the cadreization that prevailed in the Indonesian Tarbiyah movement, all ABIM teachers have to undergo a training program in order to be equipped for teaching roles (Roald 1994: 304). This manner of cadreization has facilitated more rigorous adherence to the Islamic principles propounded by ABIM.

4.1 Building the Movement

Though not often a primary focus in the social movement theory literature, leadership is critical to social movements (Nepstad and Clifford 2006). The right leadership inspires commitment, conceptualizes objectives that resonate with latent grievances, devises strategies, facilitates effective mobilization of resources and personnel, and creates and manages expectations. In this vein, scholars have noted that the influence of religious power brokers – "exemplars," as the late William Roff once described – has been growing in Southeast Asia. These actors have come to shape not just the contours of religious conservatism and activism, but also discourses of inter-religious tolerance at the national, regional, and local levels in both Indonesia and Malaysia. Apropos the earlier discussion of Islamic education, it is well established that the culture of these religious institutions lends to intimate student–teacher relationships, defined by a deep sense of obligation and obedience that often endures long after the student leaves the institution. It is imperative, then, to consider the role of leadership as part of the organizational capacity of any Islamic social movement, and also how these leaders help facilitate mobilization and transformation.

The inception of the Tarbiyah movement in Indonesia can be traced to four students who had sojourned in the Middle East: Hilmy Aminuddin, Salim Segaf al-Jufri, Abdullah Baharmus, and Encep Abdusyukur (Ahmad Norma Permata 2016: 41).[10] Upon their return to Indonesia in the 1970s, the four founded a movement dedicated to Islamic propagation and shaped it along the lines of the Ikhwanul Muslimin, with whose organizational structure, recruitment, and training and indoctrination they had grown familiar. From its inception, this movement essentially remained "shapeless" and operated "underground." It was not until 1983 that it adopted the name "Jemaah Tarbiyah," or the Tarbiyah movement (Ai Fatimah Nur Fuad 2020: 357). This early inception of the Tarbiyah movement was organized around study groups that operated as cells, as hitherto observed, "in which one mentor recruits, trains, and supervises 5–10 members, and each cell only knows each other, they do not know about other cells" (Ahmad Norma Permata 2016: 56).

Salim Segaf, who eventually emerged to be recognized as the initial leader of the Tarbiyah movement, recruited only members who were "fluent in Arabic and knowledgeable in Islamic studies" and deliberately kept the movement small and insular with little exposure to its external environment (Ahmad Norma Permata 2016: 41). This changed when Salim left for Saudi Arabia to further his studies and Hilmy Aminuddin took over the leadership role. Under Hilmy, Tarbiyah pursued a more inclusive approach to engagement by opening its membership to university students from diverse backgrounds. In some respects, this reprioritization in recruitment practice emulated what Mohamad Natsir had initiated in 1967 under the auspices of DDII when he launched a series of *dakwah* projects across university campuses under the banner of *Bina Masjid Kampus*, the earliest form of organized *tarbiyah* in modern Indonesia (Kahin 2012). As these changes within the Tarbiyah movement were taking place, because of suppressive policies enforced by the state during that period, Islamic movements like Tarbiyah began to use *tarbiyah* and *dakwah*

---

[10] Although the Muslim Brotherhood had its origins in Egypt, by the late 1960s, the government of Gamal Abdel Nasser began clamping down on them. This led to the exodus of many Brotherhood leaders and ideologues to Saudi Arabia, where they began propagating their ideas through Islamic education institutions such as the University of Madinah, where the four Indonesians studied.

programs as a means to keep an Islamist agenda alive but distanced from mainstream politics.

Under Natsir's leadership, the Salman Mosque at the Bandung Institute of Technology was to become a major hub for *dakwah* (Prayogi 2019). One of the most influential leaders to emerge from this movement was Imaduddin Abdurrachim, general secretary of the Kuwait-based International Islamic Federation of Student Organizations and, in time to come, the founder of the state-sanctioned Ikatan Cendekiawan Muslim Indonesia (Indonesian Association of Muslim Intellectuals) as well. With support from Natsir, Imaduddin established LMD, which equipped university students to undertake *dakwah* activities on campuses. This movement was also able to attract a myriad of Muslims, including many who would eventually become influential Muslim intellectuals, such as Amien Rais, a future presidential candidate and leader of the National Mandate Party, who was at one time also chairman of Muhammadiyah.

While Tarbiyah never quite took the shape of a formal organization, as a social movement it did adopt a structured approach to cadreization that was characteristic of – and indeed, inspired by – the Ikhwan. This was done for purposes of ensuring that members were fully socialized into the norms and expectations of Tarbiyah. Explaining the process of socialization, a participant in a *liqo*, the weekly meetings organized by leaders of the Tarbiyah movement, recounted:

> The leader of the *liqo* that I attended explained the principles of *liqo* stating that each member should be aware about: *ta'aruf*, *tafahum* and *takaful*. *Ta'aruf* is the first principle of *liqo* activities. Each member involved in the same *liqo* group should know each other well so as to develop interpersonal ties with the others. My experience in being involved in such a gathering showed me, for example, the importance of pretending to be a close relative of a *liqo* member in order to be easily accepted as a group member. *Liqo* members should establish close relationships in the sense of *ukhuwah* [brotherhood], by knowing the name, address and status of others in their family. Even among the members, each should know each other's psycho-logical state, way of thinking, self-capability, and economic condition. After the principle of *ta'aruf* is embedded in the psyche of the members, the second principle, which is *tafahum*, should be upheld by them. This principle of *tafahum* or "understanding" consists of three factors that can strengthen relationships among the members. They are, (1) strengthening love and compassion for each other, (2) negating hatred that can break relationships and, (3) avoiding dispute among the members. And the last principle which is considered to be the result of the process of *ta'aruf* and *tafahum*, is that of *takaful* [responsibility to each other]. This principle implies that every

member looks after the others, particularly when one of the members faces difficulties. (Ahmad Ali Nurdin 2011: 342)

Liqo further proved an invaluable vehicle for recruitment and mobilization for another reason. At a time when the New Order regime pursued a repressive approach towards Islamic movements, the informal structure of *liqo* ensured that these mechanisms eluded the attention of the state, even as the movement gradually built up its networked base. The robustness of this organized strategy of cadreization would later pay dividends when Tarbiyah spawned a political party, the PKS. That the party managed to retain a significant degree of coherence despite challenges that would confront it as internal tensions surfaced between ideologues and pragmatists, or as a result of corruption scandals, can largely be attributed to the strong grassroots organizational structure and foundation upon which Tarbiyah was built (Kramer 2014).

It was by way of this orientation toward a more strategic and comprehensive recruitment strategy that Tarbiyah succeeded in attracting new members and expanding its branches to various major cities across the country. These new members represented a diverse demography of individuals, which included neourbanites and students, as well as professionals. Notably, Tarbiyah managed also to attract members from other Islamic organizations and movements, such as Salafi groups, NU, Muhammadiyah, DDII, and Himpunan Mahasiswa Islam (HMI) (Yon Machmudi 2008). Tarbiyah also grew in popularity among students and professionals who flocked to urban centers from rural areas in search of education and employment opportunities. For these rural Muslims displaced for economic reasons, membership in Tarbiyah played an important role beyond merely an expression of religious piety; it also served the social function of addressing the dislocation created by the relocation to urban centers. It was for all these reasons that, although the Tarbiyah movement was compelled by circumstances to remain underground, by the 1990s, it "had stable networks in many universities in major cities across the country, and it started taking over intra-curricular and extra-curricular student organizations" (Ahmad Norma Permata 2016: 42).

4.2 A Transnational Dimension

Tarbiyah leaders played an instrumental role in establishing and cultivating crucial transnational links that were shaped and nourished by the growing contact between Indonesian students and their Ikhwanul Muslimin counterparts, mostly in Saudi Arabia, where members of the movement had taken refuge following the crackdown by the Egyptian military regime. Efforts by Indonesian Islamist intellectual leaders such as Natsir – who by virtue of his role as Indonesian representative to the World Muslim League in the 1950s managed to procure scholarships for Indonesian students through connections he built with Saudi elites and the Egyptian government – catalyzed this process. Through these efforts, such leaders played a key role in establishing intellectual circles receptive to the transmission of *tarbiyah* ideas from the Middle East.

Concomitantly, the growing contact between Indonesian Islamist circles and the Ikhwanul Muslimin hastened the circulation of the "practical vision" of *tarbiyah* between the Middle East and Indonesia and precipitated the propagation of Ikhwan ideas that Tarbiyah scholars translated for use in university campuses, as well as in *usrah* that were by then mushrooming across Indonesia. By dint of this "Saudi factor," manifested in the circulation of Indonesian students, scholarships, and translated literature between Saudi Arabia and Indonesia (Java in particular), especially in the 1970s and 1980s – including the four Saudi-educated founders of the movement mentioned previously – an Islamist program would emerge from Tarbiyah as it positioned itself as a comprehensive political ideology and alternative to the New Order regime. According to Yon Machmudi, "the interaction of Indonesian students with ideas of the Muslim Brothers in Saudi Arabia persuaded them of the importance of a multi-dimensional struggle for Islam. Islam was not confined within a practice [but as a comprehensive ideology] ... encompassed all political, economic, social, and cultural dimensions of the human being' (Yon Machmudi 2008: 151).

The circulation of Ikhwan ideas was further facilitated by a massive publication and translation enterprise that became a definitive part of the Tarbiyah movement. The totality of the impact of translated texts regarding *tarbiyah* on intellectual or student circles in Indonesia cannot be overemphasized. Yon Machmudi notes that "since 1998, the beginning of the post-Soeharto or Reformation era, it is no exaggeration to say that hundreds of books about the Muslim Brothers' thought and history have been printed and have enjoyed popular acclaim" (Yon Machmudi 2008: 151); indeed, this might be reflective of the decades-long trend of Indonesian intellectual circles drawing upon "practical visions" of *tarbiyah* to both critique and explain their sociopolitical worlds.

At any rate, the circulation of *tarbiyah* ideals has undeniably increased with the proliferation of Islamic printing houses in Indonesia in the immediate post– New Order era, allowing Indonesians unrestricted access to the works of Islamist intellectuals such as Hasan al-Banna, Syed Qutb, and Abdul A'la Maududi, all of whom propagated Islam as a comprehensive political ideology against military dictatorships and secular regimes. These publishing houses include the Era Intermedia Publishers, which has published *al-Ma'thurat*

(Hassan al-Banna's collection of daily prayers) and *Risalah Pergerakan* (a collection of Hassan al-Banna's sermons and lectures) and "sold more than 60,000 and 30,000 copies respectively" in the period of political transition (Yon Machmudi 2008: 153). The Tarbiyah movement, and later PKS, became a permanent client of these publishing houses in post–New Order Indonesia as it actively distributed published materials pertaining to *tarbiyah* to a far wider audience than previously, when Tarbiyah predominantly confined its efforts to campuses in Java.

4.3 Organizations, Networks, and State Engagement

By comparison with the Tarbiyah movement, which was more diffused, furtive, and inclined to keep the Indonesian state at a safe remove, even as a social movement, Dakwah in Malaysia for the most part revolved around established organizations. Some of these organizations worked fairly closely with the Malaysian state, such as ABIM, IRC, and IKRAM (Pertubuhan Ikram Malaysia), although others, like Darul Arqam and Jemaat Tabligh, operated at the margins. The institutional identity of these organizations presented opportunities for coordination of community development and Islamic outreach programs with each other, and sometimes with state religious and welfare organizations. Such combined efforts provided a more expansive base through which the propagation of ideas and mobilization could be facilitated in a more structured fashion and, unlike for Tarbiyah in Indonesia, unhindered by excessive concern for the prospects of state repression (Mohd Anuar Tahir 1993: 9). Describing the dynamics of cooperation within the Dakwah movement, Ahmad Fauzi observed:

> In the formative phase of Islamic resurgence in the 1970s, despite the emergence of several Islamic groups operating under different organizational and leadership structures, Dakwah was regarded as a distinctive socio-religious movement in itself. Inter-relationships among the groups were considered unproblematic, and even membership among them was described as flexible and inter-changeable. Distant co-operation was observed during these initial years, especially in public activities involving members of all groups. Similarly, one group's evaluation of current affairs was not too different from another's, as reflected in the concurrent flavor of their statements. The authorities consequently felt threatened by an apparently monolithic force of Islamists from diverse backgrounds. (Ahmad Fauzi Abdul Hamid 2003: 59–60)

Notwithstanding the more visible and structured nature of a large part of the Malaysian Dakwah movement, as for Tarbiyah in Indonesia, leadership has played a crucial role in efforts to expand its popularity. ABIM, the largest and most established organization in the Dakwah movement, was led by a number of prominent intellectuals and activists. In fact, many of them would go on to assume leadership roles in other Islamic organizations, state bodies, and even political parties after cutting their teeth in ABIM. *Primus inter pares* among this generation was Anwar Ibrahim, who led ABIM through the 1970s and into the early 1980s. Under Anwar and against the backdrop of the revival of Islamic consciousness among Malaysian Muslims, ABIM assumed the role of critic of the Malaysian government, frequently protesting state policies for their alleged lack of Islamic character and virtue. Anwar was aided in this effort by able lieutenants such as Fadzil Noor, Abdul Hadi Awang, Ismail Mina, Kamarudin Mohd Nor, Othman Bakar, Sanusi Junid, and Nakhaie Ahmad, who became household names themselves as their writings and speeches framed intellectual discussions of Islamic precepts that took place in the ubiquitous *usrah*, and which, in turn, anchored and accelerated political mobilization through the vehicle of student associations (Sidek Baba 1991). Both Fadzil Noor and Hadi Awang would later assume leadership of PAS. Of note is the fact that Hadi Awang was a student of the famed Syrian Ikhwan scholar Said Hawwa in the University of Madinah; Ikhwan ideas would resonate in Hadi Awang's later intellectual positions and writings (Khatib 2012: 53). For instance, in his book, *Muqadimmah Aqidah Muslimin* (Introduction to the Creed of Muslims), Hadi Awang argues, in similar fashion to Sayyid Qutb, the validity of discrediting as infidels Muslims who are deemed not to be practicing or protecting the faith (Abdul Hadi Awang 1985; Liow 2009: 37–39).

Following the departure of Anwar and his generation of charismatic activists, leadership of ABIM passed through a new generation of accomplished Islamic thinkers, including Siddik Fadil, Mohd Nur Monutty, Yusri Mohamad, Sidek Baba, and Saari Sungib (who would also later lead IRC and JIM). This subsequent cohort of ABIM leaders were less firebrand but no less effective when it came to building the organization. Under them, ABIM gravitated away from the overt political engagement characteristic of the Anwar era toward welfare and charitable causes, many of which they pursued in collaboration with the Malaysian state. Massive antigovernment rallies, prevalent under Anwar's leadership, gave way to lower-key, more considered employment of the time-honored institution of the *usrah* and the cadreization process it facilitated, through which ABIM made efforts to align organization policy thinking with state policies. It stands to reason, however, that this alignment was less about any fundamental change in ABIM's principles than the fact that one of its own – none other than Anwar – was now in the corridors of power, by virtue of having been recruited into the UMNO establishment and given a cabinet position. Through that position, Anwar could effect changes that ABIM was agitating for, not to mention drawing former ABIM compatriots into the political establishment, from which they, too, could shape national policies decisively.

The cadreization and mobilization that took place through the mechanism of *usrah* centered on the preponderance of *dakwah* literature made available through an active translation and publication industry in Malaysia. Curiously, much of this "original" literature itself came in the form of translations. This is because many of the standard *dakwah* texts that arrived in Malaysia were in fact English translations of original Arabic texts, a result of a massive translation and dissemination enterprise bankrolled by Saudi Arabia through its petrodollars. By the late 1980s and early 1990s, a cottage industry had emerged in Malaysia that translated the works of Hassan al-Banna, Syed Qutb, Yusuf Qaradawi, Muhammad Asad, Abu A'la Maududi, Fathi Yakan, and many other renowned Islamic thinkers. ABIM, in particular, created an extensive book-publishing program, through which it churned out "a great variety of inexpensive educational, informational, and sometime polemical literature, much of it translated into Malay from other languages" (Roff 1998: 226–227). Aside from the publication enterprise associated with groups like ABIM, independent presses, including the occasional unlicensed one, also emerged especially in Kelantan and Kuala Lumpur to produce their own, easily accessible Islamic studies material. Several key texts came to be especially popular in Dakwah *usrah* circles, including *To Be a Muslim* (Fathi Yakan), *Milestones* (Syed Qutb), and *al-Mathurat* (Hassan al-Banna). Locally produced scholarship supplemented this Islamic studies canon. Among the more popular of these works was *Risalah Usrah* by Abu 'Urwah (the pen name of Saari Sungib, former president of JIM but also previously from ABIM), which mapped a template for an *usrah* curriculum (Mohamed Imran Mohamed Taib 2012). Other Dakwah groups in Malaysia replicated his ABIM model of recruitment and mobilization through texts and study. The IRC, for instance, and later JIM as well, also set great store by the role of the *usrah* in cadreization and indoctrination, to the extent of publishing their own *tarbiyah* materials to use in their study circles.

Another notable feature of ABIM was its establishment of overseas branches and student organizations (such as the Malaysia Islamic Study Group that proliferated in North America and Australia) as it reached out to the community of Malaysian students studying abroad. These overseas branches also facilitated active expressions of solidarity with the *ummah* around global causes, among the more prominent being Palestine and the Bosnian conflict, and provided additional avenues through which Islamist ideas and movements emanating from abroad shaped the Dakwah organization. The IRC too, modeled its organizational structure after the Ikhwan, to which its founding leaders, such as Saari Sungib, Khalid Samad, and Nizar Jamaluddin, were exposed; they internalized the organizational principles and mobilizing strategies of the Egyptian movement as students in Britain. Both IRC and its later incarnation, JIM, relied heavily on *dakwah* and *tarbiyah* for the *islah* (reform) programs on which their organizational identity and mobilizing capacity were predicated (Saari Sungib 1994). Similar to ABIM, JIM also created a network of kindergartens and private Islamic schools, which they managed under Musleh Venture Berhad, and expanded the organization's visibility through various public engagement programs (Maszlee Malik and Hamidah Mat 2014: 112–113).

As suggested earlier, ABIM and IRC initially cooperated closely. In fact, many of the first generation of IRC members who returned from Britain joined ABIM seamlessly, and after IRC established a presence in Malaysia, members of both organizations interacted freely. This affiliation diminished, however, when Anwar left ABIM to join UMNO, and subsequently, when IRC perceived ABIM to be equivocating on its erstwhile-robust approach toward emplacing Islamic strictures in Malaysia.

4.4 The Digital Frontier

One of the most striking developments in recent years has been how an emergent digital domain comprising information and communication technologies and so-called new media has come to assume a greater role in the expression of religious identity among Muslims in Indonesia and Malaysia. In brief, this digital domain refers to the landscape that new, interactive media platforms occupy, platforms that can disseminate information swiftly. These include social network platforms such as Facebook, Twitter, and Instagram; instant messaging platforms like SnapChat, WhatsApp, and Telegram; video platforms like YouTube and vlogs; and of course, websites. While the Tarbiyah and Dakwah movements considered here predate the internet age, advancements in technology over time have transformed the communications and media landscape in which they operate, and they have had to respond accordingly. Enabled by technological advancements as well as growth in internet penetration and smartphone usage in Indonesia and Malaysia, these platforms have opened up novel channels for the transmission and propagation of ideas and offered up new avenues for recruitment and mobilization through which Islamic social movements in both Indonesia and Malaysia have extended their reach.

In view of this new landscape, scholarship on Islamic social movements must take into account the role of new media and information communication technology. In 2001, Peter Mandaville considered the growth of information technology and how it impacted Muslim lives by globalizing their world and creating new conceptions of Islamic identity and community in terms of time, space, and meaning (Mandaville 2001). Meanwhile, Gary Bunt studied the cyber world of Muslims by exploring an online community of jihadi discourses, imams, and fatwas, and how cyberspace was shaping Islam in the digital era. Bunt went on to further study the role of Muslim groups online and how these virtual communities were shaping discussions on Islam in the contemporary Muslim world (Bunt 2003, 2009). The main contention of this scholarship is that new media have shaped how Muslims, and, in particular, the Muslim middle class, approach traditional religious practices such as Qur'anic readings and discussions, the giving and receiving of charity, and consumption of religious preaching. In Indonesia, the advent of new and social media has brought about the emergence of a new generation of Islamic preachers who are gaining popularity in various Tarbiyah-related networks regionally and, increasingly, nationally, as well (Wahyuddin Halim 2018).

A signal feature of the digital domain is its decentralized nature. Given the difficulties inherent in regulating this domain, it stands to reason that several challenges would emerge. Indeed, it is this concern that begets research on online radicalization and extremist and terrorist groups, research that has proliferated with the advent of ISIS and their grandiose claims and acts of terror. At the same time, this domain is also an arena in which competing claims to authenticity and authority play out as a function of the convergence between the unregulated nature of this digital and new media landscape and divergent expressions of Islamic identity that often define Muslim communities in Indonesia and Malaysia. As Mustaqim Pabbajah and others argue in the case of Indonesia:

> It is not an exaggeration to say that Indonesia is the most difficult Muslim country to answer the question about who actually is the sole owner of religious authority to regulate and give direction to Muslims to translate Islamic messages in life. Moreover, in a new media based society ... where the public is increasingly scattered both socially and intellectually, it can hardly determine who owns religious authority and what the limits are. (Mustaqim Pabbajah et al. 2019: 6)

The larger point, however, is how *dakwah* and *tarbiyah* have migrated into the digital domain, affording Islamic social movements new vehicles for education, outreach, and mass mobilization in the name of Islam, as movement actors and leaders (or, as it were, social-media publicity teams) seek to create an "online *ummah*" where like-minded individuals are able to identify with similar communities online, even as they also distinguish themselves from other communities (Irwandani 2016). It is for this reason that Bart Barendregt observes that "late modernity in an Indonesian context increasingly has become defined in terms of technological innovation. For many urban Indonesians, modernity has also become equivalent to mobility, and this includes physical and social mobility but especially the eye-catching use of mobile media" (Barendregt 2008: 160). He concludes that the digital domain has managed to "domesticate, Indonesianize, and Islamize" Indonesian society (Barendregt 2008: 161).

Needless to say, there is also a demographic dimension at work, given that digital and new-media activism tends to appeal to younger Muslims, the same constituents that the Tarbiyah and Dakwah movements target. By this token, a report carried in Kompasiana (2018) has argued that in Indonesia, the growing popularity of digital space in the propagation of religious ideas and ideals can be explained by the fact that the internet is fast becoming the primary source of religious knowledge for young Indonesians, for whom spiritual guidance is derived more from online sources than from traditional sources like the mosque. As Nilan and Mansfield (2014: 6) observe:

> Many kinds of spaces are significant in the lives of young urban Indonesians. Not only are physical places important, but also the virtual spaces accessible through mobile phone and internet technology. These new technologies enable communication, information sharing and networking. In both public and virtual spaces, young people can collectively connect with the cultures and political agendas of a world brought closer by the pressures of globalization, even while they give priority to the local; to their friends, siblings, and cousins.

A similar trend is evident in Malaysia, where youths also prefer to obtain news and religious opinions and rulings from online sources rather than from traditional sources (Freeman 2013).

Considering the growing popularity of the internet, it should hardly be surprising to find Islamic movements and parties engaging digital and new-media platforms to mobilize, recruit, and propagate their ideas (Nurdin Rusli 2013). Scholars have already identified how Islamist parties in Indonesia and Malaysia have employed networked communications using the internet and social-media platforms, for purposes of expanding their reach to new generations of potential cadre (Muhammad Syahban Siddiq et al. 2011). At a rudimentary level, these media have provided a means through which information can be disseminated more quickly, thereby enabling more effective mobilization for events and even protests, as evident in the call to rally in protest during the Jakarta gubernatorial elections in 2016 and in support of an antipornography bill in 2017. At a more sophisticated level, new communication platforms have been used to enhance *dakwah* efforts. For instance, Eva Nisa has described how the Tarbiyah movement introduced WhatsApp as a vehicle for *dakwah* by encouraging reading of the Qur'an through a program called One Day One Juz (ODOJ):

> sometime in 2013 [Tarbiyah activist] Nurkholifa began to use WhatsApp to report to her murabbiyah [religious mentor] about her daily recitations of the Qur'an (tilawah yaumiyyah). Within the tradition of the Tarbiyah movement, a pupil or mutarabbi (m)/ mutarabbiyah (f) of a halaqah (religious study circle), who is supervised by a murabbi or murabbiyah, has to report his or her weekly performances of acts of devotion – including reciting the Qur'an daily. Tarbiyah mentors utilise a checklist to monitor the progress of daily religious activities conducted by their members. Tilawah or reciting the Qur'an is one of the activities listed in each individualised programme, otherwise known as mutaba'ah yaumiyah. This means that each member of the Tarbiyah movement should recite the Qur'an. (Nisa 2018: 28)

Specifically, because this program encouraged Tarbiyah cadre to report their *tilawah yaumiyyah* (daily recitations of the Qur'an) to their *murabbi* (mentor), 'ODOJ initially served as an important means of strengthening the identity and fellowship of cadres and activists of the Tarbiyah movement' (Nisa 2018: 28).

Consonant with observable patterns in Indonesia, digital and new media have also gained currency in the efforts of Dakwah movement organizations and Islamist political parties in Malaysia to expand their base, indicating that, even in the act of *dakwah*, "religion is often politicized by new media" (Aini Maznina Manaf 2018: 126). Yet at the same time, there are distinctions to be drawn in comparison to Indonesia, including that, although cyberspace is difficult to regulate, in Malaysia, state religious authorities have been far more effective in policing this domain than their Indonesian counterparts. Case in point is how the Malaysian authorities regulate fatwa (legal opinion) issuance, so much so that while issuing online fatwa is a growing trend not only in Indonesia, but across the Muslim world, this practice has been closely policed in Malaysia (Abd. Hadi Borham 2018: 58).

All said, it should be remembered that Islamist social movements in both Indonesia and Malaysia essentially cut their teeth building community networks based on the Ikhwan-inspired, *usrah*-centered formula of cadreization predicated on very personal relationships. Concomitantly, the impersonal nature of digital and new media suggests that, while they provide useful additional vehicles to reach out to members and potential members, the intimacy of the connection makes grassroots mobilization still the cornerstone of Islamist social movements' organizational capacity.

5 The Foray into Politics

The previous two sections established the key ideas Islamic social movements have advocated in Indonesia and Malaysia since the late 1960s, and how these ideas found institutional expression as the organizing principles for structured programs designed for purposes of mobilization, recruitment, and expanded influence. Having addressed the substance of these Islamic social movements and how they mobilize in order to advance their goals and objectives, we now turn to political participation and the evolving socioreligious and political landscape – enabling political opportunity structures, in the lexicon of social movement theory – in both Indonesia and Malaysia.

From the mid-1980s onward, the relationship between the state and Islam in Indonesia underwent a transformation as the New Order shifted to a more accommodating approach toward public expressions of religiosity. By then, Suharto himself had initiated several projects that not only underscored this turn but also bolstered his personal credentials as a Muslim political leader. These included the creation of a quasi-state foundation, the Yayasan Amal Bakti Muslim Pancasila (YAMP), in 1982 to oversee the enhancement of visible Islamic infrastructure across the country. Within a decade, YAMP was able to collect IDR830 million (approximately USD58,000) in tithes and contributions, more than half of which was used to build in excess of 400 mosques throughout the country (Bahtiar Effendy 2003: 168). Following advice from Majelis Ulama Indonesia, or Indonesia Ulama Council, a substantial portion of the funds was also directed toward the building of an Islamic bank and dispatching of Islamic missionaries to remote areas across the archipelago to perform *dakwah*.

As an expression of changes in political opportunity structures and the social and political conditions they create, this gradual shift in dynamics between the state and Islam, and the relaxation of hitherto-stringent policies toward the expression of religiosity, paved the way for the Tarbiyah movement to expand its activities and introduce its *dakwah* to a wider audience beyond university campuses, in broader society. The result echoes what Jillian Schwedler noted in Yemen: "If an authoritarian regime decides to initiate a process of limited political liberalization, the new opportunities increase the likelihood that new forms of mobilization will emerge to take advantage of changing political conditions" (Schwedler 2004: 205–206). In particular, the authoritarian regime may "open the political system" so that civil society organizations and political parties can deliberate issues and debate in a public/political arena (Schwedler 2004: 205–206). The Tarbiyah movement experienced this dynamic as it embarked on practical and organized civil society activism to support social welfare by establishing Islamic education institutions and medical facilities.

Within Tarbiyah circles, this period became known as *mihwar sha'bi*, or "the popular phase," in which "Tarbiyah members who were trained in the previous period were now required to interact with the wider society and to take part in educating society (*al-irsyad almujtama'*)" (Ai Fatimah Nur Fuad 2017: 146, 168). Ai Fatimah Nur Fuad further elaborates on how Tarbiyah cadres were expected to operate in this climate of greater openness; her observations are worth citing here at length:

> Tarbiyah members who already had distinctive Tarbiyah characteristics (*tamayuz*) were expected by the leaders to spread and conduct nonverbal *dakwah* among Indonesian society. Verbal *dakwah* here involves a call to religious piety which, according to the movement, is achieved by members providing themselves as role models for society, as indicated by a statement from a leader of the Tarbiyah movement: There is guidance (*kaidah*) that (members) should always be reminded (of): all of us (Tarbiyah members) must interact with anybody with our Islamic "uniqueness" (fa-*l yakhtalithuun wa-laakin yatamayyazuun*). This guidance does not require the members to be exclusive, but (to be) blended within the society without losing their "uniqueness." (Ai Fatimah Nur Fuad 2017: 169)

As discussed in Section 4.3, the opportunity for more effective mobilization was also occasioned by the robust growth of a publishing industry that flourished in the late 1980s and early1990s. During this period, publishing houses associated with the Tarbiyah movement, such as Rabbani Press, Asyshamil, and Intermedia, gained greater prominence when they accelerated their outreach activities and proliferated across Indonesia, while various *dakwah*-related outreach programs were advanced by Tarbiyah organizations such as Sekolah Dasar Islam Terpadu- SDIT, Lembaga Dakwah Sekolah-LDS, and Lembaga Dakwah Kampus-LDK, as Tarbiyah gradually expanded its visibility in Indonesian society.

This process of increasingly open engagement in the affairs of the day accelerated in the wake of events of 1998 that proved to be a watershed for the Islamist movement in Indonesia. The political landscape underwent radical change, and new opportunities for political mobilization emerged. As mass demonstrations gathered pace and Reformasi brought thirty-two years of authoritarian rule toward a dramatic close, Tarbiyah lent their voices to calls for Suharto's resignation. The New Order, which began in 1966 when Suharto replaced Sukarno as president of Indonesia, came to an end on May 21, 1998 with the resignation of Suharto under conditions of grave national economic duress. The end of the New Order paved the way for a new era defined in part by the contemplation and articulation of ideas such as freedom of expression and public deliberation, all integral elements of an incipient Indonesian democracy.

In response to the opening of political space, various movements and organiza-tions came forward with their own aspirations to play defining roles in shaping post–New Order Indonesia. Needless to say, this surge included Islamist move-ments, and Tarbiyah stood at the forefront. Replicating the Ikhwan experience, the Tarbiyah movement had become not just an agent of religious reform, but, gradually, a political force that mobilized as a "united force of ummah regard-less of individual religious orientations" (Yon Machmudi 2008: 4). Essentially, Tarbiyah's transnational ideas, already circulating between Indonesia and the Middle East through the efforts of Indonesian students returning from Egypt in the 1970s and 1980s who "brought back Brotherhood [Ikhwan] ideas on movement tactics and organization" (Hefner 2009: 74), had the effect of allowing a systematic buildup of the Islamic activist base. That growth eventu-ally seeded the proliferation of Islamic movements that sought to shape the post–New Order political climate in the early days of the Reformasi era.[11]

5.1 From Tarbiyah to PKS

As Reformasi gathered pace, Tarbiyah activists already occupied leadership positions in student executive bodies as an outcome of prevailing movement strategies of mobilization. From that vantage, they began to control student governments at university and faculty levels, often shunting aside candidates from other Muslim organizations. The movement also extended its influence in the Forum Silaturahmi Lembaga Dakwah Kampus (FSLDK or Forum for Coordinating Campus Predication), an extracampus proselytization network that encompassed several secular universities across Indonesia. Through FSLDK, Tarbiyah activists were able to establish Kesatuan Aksi Mahasiswa Muslim Indonesia (KAMMI or Indonesian Muslim Student Action Union) in 1998, which in turn provided an avenue for the cadre of Tarbiyah to become active agents in the mass protests that eventually led to the resignation of President Suharto. Tarbiyah activism, through the vehicle of KAMMI, would later evolve into a bona fide political organization initially known as Partai Keadilan or PK, which would later morph into the PKS. As Natsir pithily described, "Before we used politics as a way to preach, now we use preaching as a way to engage in politics" (Lukman Hakiem and Tansil Linrung 1997: 7). Indeed, this was what PKS attempted to achieve, by way of what it deemed to be a natural progression from personal piety to political participation. The litmus case of a transformation from social movement to political party, PKS would

---

[11] It is important to note that not all the Islamic/Islamist movements were outgrowths from the Tarbiyah movement, but neither were they overnight phenomena; they merely now had their moment with the end of authoritarianism.

rise to prominence post New Order not only for its performance at the polls, but also for the manner in which it negotiated sociopolitical space according to its own peculiar understandings and interpretations of, and struggles over, how an Islamist party should function in a working democracy, in the process cementing its place in the landscape of party politics.

The transformation of the Tarbiyah movement into a political party was justified as a new phase of *dakwah* – known in the lexicon as *"mihwar mu'assasi"* (the political penetration phase) or *"al-'am al-intikhabi* (the election period)" (Ai Fatimah Nur Fuad 2017: 171). As explained in official Tarbiyah documents:

> These years are years for struggle to strengthen the existence of our political movement for the sake of *dakwah, al wujud al-siyasi li al-dakwah* (the political necessity of *dakwah*) in this era, all cadres should become voters and constituents in the wider society. The cadres should perform their *dakwah* and politics in order to gain love and sympathy (of the society) so that they are able join the Tarbiyah movement (and support the party). (Ai Fatimah Nur Fuad 2017: 172)

Ai Fatimah Nur Fuad explains the process through which Tarbiyah leadership decided to embark on the path of mainstream political participation:

> In 1998, Anis Matta, a key leader of the Tarbiyah movement (the former President of PKS from 2013 to 2015 and a long serving secretary general of the party, from 1998 to 2013), asked ... Tarbiyah activists whether or not they wanted to enter the political arena. There was a voting process to see the interests of activists in politics. The vote showed that about 76% wanted to struggle through politics, while the rest wanted to remain with their *dakwah* movement. The majority agreed to enter politics because they wanted to contribute (to developing) a better society – *ishlah al-ummah*. We held an internal meeting among the Tarbiyah cadres in order to review this result and to decide the next plan. Alhamdulillah (praise to Allah) through *takbirullah* (Allah's guidance) and *takdirullah* (Allah's predestination), we entered the political arena. This moment, for us, was a stage of our maturity to understand the *manhaj* (the overall ideology) of our *dakwah*. (Ai Fatimah Nur Fuad 2017: 172)

Though Tarbiyah decided to evolve a political program to enter the political arena after much deliberation and with wide internal support, the decision was not without detractors from within. Specifically, ideological purists among its ranks resisted the move, such as Abu Ridho and Yusuf Supendi, who took the view that Tarbiyah should eschew politics and stay true to the "apolitical" mission of *dakwah* (Ahmad Norma Permata 2016: 243–246). Others, such as Anis Matta, Hidayat Nur Wahid, and Ihsan Tanjung, while principally in agreement regarding the need to progress to formal politics, were nevertheless of the view that the timing (the late 1990s) was premature, and that Tarbiyah should bide its time and invest in further development of human resources, political networks, and financial capacity before transitioning into mainstream politics (Noor Firman 2015: 113). At any rate, the internal referendum nullified such reticence and opposition, revealing overwhelming support for the move to form an official political party, including from luminaries such as Rahmat Abdullah, who went by the moniker "Sheikh of the Tarbiyah" (Irfun Teguh 2018).

Hardly unique to PKS, such tension between ideologues and pragmatists would persist even after the formation of the political party. Indeed, they would manifest in debates over policy issues and political candidates. For instance, in the buildup to the presidential election of 2004, the party had a faction – led by party chairman Hidayat Nur Wahid – that supported Amien Rais and another – led by Party Secretary-General Anies Matta – that supported the candidature of General Wiranto. The issue at hand was the Islamic credentials of the respective candidates, as well as whether to prioritize a candidate with a more nationalist or Islamic agenda. The debate was rehearsed in the second round of the presidential election, as party factions found themselves exercised over whether to support the eventual winner, Susilo Bambang Yudhoyono. Whereas some in the party leadership advocated support for Yudhoyono and his "Islamo-democrat" agenda, other Islamists within the party opposed the decision in the belief that Yudhoyono was a secularist who opposed the implementation of Islamic law. Following the decision to enter the arena of mainstream politics, Tarbiyah mandated that members would automatically be conferred membership in the political party; those who refused risked expulsion. In the event, those who fell in the latter category left to join other movements that eschewed mainstream political engagement, such as the Hizbut Tahrir and various Salafi groups, through which they could continue their labors in *dakwah*, which they prioritized over political participation.

Over a period of two decades following the turbulent years of Reformasi, PKS has managed to gain a foothold in Indonesian society and occupies "an *avant-garde* position in the configuration of post–New Order Islamism and has developed relatively systematic discourses and counter-discourses on democracy through its own far-reaching media and publications" (Masdar Hilmy 2009: 5). Its Tarbiyah intellectual roots though, remain palpable in internal party narratives that stress "practical ideas," which include the notion of "re-Islamizing" society by stressing economic, social, and political developments that would benefit the wider Muslim community. Simply put, PKS marks "the pole that seeks intra-parliamentary means to promote Islam through democracy" (Masdar Hilmy 2009: 5). Moreover, in a marked departure from the Saudi brand of Islam that shuns the Sufi basis of *tarbiyah* and the Ikhwan model of engagement it spawned, PKS consciously attempts to "return to" reformist Sufi practices of Hassan al-Banna, including *halqa, daura, pengajian* (religious lectures), *liqa* (meetings), *rihla* (tours), *mabit* (overnight stays), seminars, and workshops, reconciling these practices with prevailing Indonesian cultural mores (Noorhaidi Hasan 2009: 14). Further demonstrating localization of *tarbiyah* in the mainstream Javanese context, PKS has, for the most part, displayed a disposition that is comfortable with cultural accommodation, legitimizing these concessions as being in line with the *tarbiyah* spirit of "moderation" predicated on *Haqiqa Sufiyya* or "Sufi reality/truth." This principle, associated with Hassan al-Banna and one that PKS is fond of repeating, speaks to how traditional Sufi *tarikat* (orders) play celebrated roles as peacemakers and mediators (Hassan al-Banna 2001; Ali Abdul Halim Mahmud 2004).

5.2 Malaysian Dakwah and Political Engagement

In a way not dissimilar from Indonesia, events at the turn of the century contrived to offer critical opportunities for Islamic social movements in Malaysia to accelerate efforts to shape developments in the country by means of deeper engagement in mainstream politics. This process had its roots in what scholars have identified as an Islamization process traceable to the early 1970s and attributable in no small measure to the emergence of the Dakwah movement. This resurgence of Islamic consciousness and piety coincided with a shift in national discourse and policy to the advantage of the Malay-Muslim community when, after the national trauma of the May 13, 1969 race riots, Malaysian society underwent a fundamental reorganization with the introduction of affirmative-action policies that favored the Malay-Muslim community in the political, economic, and cultural spheres, and that mainstreamed Islam in all domains of Malay political, social and economic life, so much so that by the 1980s, Islamization all but became unofficial state policy. Put differently, "if previously Islam was mainly expressed in symbolic terms, especially in relation to the institution of the royalty and popular Malay culture, the government's efforts drew Islam into the heart of all economic and noneconomic life" (Shamsul 1997: 210).

UMNO's Islamization policy first found form in a greater emphasis on Islamic culture and education. By the 1980s, the program extended beyond the cultural and educational sphere to encompass economics, with the introduction of Islamic banking, the proliferation of Waqf (Islamic foundations), and an attempt by the government of Mahathir Mohamad to articulate a Muslim work ethic to underpin his industrialization program for the country, as well as to inform its foreign policy as Malaysia emerged on the global stage as a vocal champion for Muslim causes globally. To lend weight to this state-driven effort, the religious bureaucracy, a hitherto minor arm of the state, saw its standing enhanced, budget increased, and staffing inflated with Islamic studies graduates produced by local universities, the cauldron of *dakwah* activism and beneficiaries of affirmative-action programs of the New Education Policy, which was the education-policy component of the more comprehensive New Economic Policy.

As alluded to in Section 3.2, one of the defining events in the transformation from social movement to mainstream politics was undoubtedly Anwar Ibrahim's move to join UMNO in 1982. Considered the embodiment of the Dakwah movement by way of his reputation as an activist, thinker, and mobilizer, Anwar personified its turn to politics when he was courted by both UMNO and PAS. His decision to leave ABIM to satisfy a growing political ambition marked a consequential turning point in the history of Islamic social movements in Malaysia and the genesis of their transformation into a force in mainstream politics. For a start, Anwar's departure precipitated those of several prominent ABIM colleagues as well. These included Fadzil Noor, Abdul Hadi Awang, and Nakhaie Ahmad, all of whom joined PAS (Nakhaie would eventually switch to UMNO). To be sure, prominent movement leaders were not the only ones who ventured into the waters of party politics. A large segment of the rank and file followed them as well, joining either PAS or UMNO. Second, Anwar's departure also led to a shift away from the more open, confrontational style that characterized ABIM activism and mobilization under Anwar's leadership to a more conciliatory approach that his successors began pursuing toward the state.

With this more symbiotic relationship, ABIM members began filling the ranks of the UMNO-led government as they aligned their objectives for Islamic-oriented development with the state's, in the process building "an influential network in the political structure with significant impact on state policies" (Mohd Kamal Hassan 2003: 105). After all, now that their standard bearer was in government, there was great incentive to work with, rather than against, the state. Meanwhile, the Mahathir government's recruitment of Anwar was also, on its part, a function of a larger plan to absorb elements of the Dakwah movement to head off the political challenge from PAS.

Third, led by Anwar, the influx of ABIM members into UMNO also began to change the complexion of the party and the government it led. Whereas the party remained ardent Malay nationalists, its program increasingly took on a more Islamic flavor as the influence of Anwar – and by extension, the Dakwah movement – began to grow. This further coincided with Mahathir's announcement that he would "Islamize the government machinery," a move that he proceeded to explain during an interview with *Utusan Melayu* in 1984:

> What we mean by Islamization is the inculcation of Islamic values in government. Such an inculcation is not the same as the implementation of Islamic laws in the country. Islamic laws are for Muslims and meant for their personal laws but the laws of the nation, although not Islamic-based, can be used as long as they do not come into conflict with Islamic principles. (quoted in Yeoh 2014: 161)

The role that Anwar Ibrahim played in this Islamization process warrants amplification. As a cabinet minister, Anwar oversaw the introduction of the *Penerapan Nilai-nilai Islam* (Inculcation of Islamic Values) framework of governance that the Mahathir administration sought to apply across the government. This led to the establishment of various levers of Islamic influence over society that the state would wield, in domains like law (specifically, empowering the Shari'a Court), banking and finance, education, and the development of JAKIM, a federal entity empowered to safeguard the place of Islam as the religion of the Malaysian Federation. As education minister, and ably assisted by former Dakwah colleagues such as Sidek Baba, Anwar was instrumental in introducing a moral education program in schools that centered on religion and focused primarily on Islamic civilization. This built on earlier policies Mahathir introduced in 1974, when he was himself education minister, and enhanced the pipeline of Islamic studies graduates who would benefit from government scholarships to advance their education. As recipients of government scholarships, these graduates would eventually populate a public service that came to prioritize applicants with strong Islamic backgrounds. In Ikhwanesque fashion, they would become the vanguard of the Islamization policies that Mahathir's government introduced, effecting change from within. Moreover, because of Anwar's relationships and connections with Islamic social movements, they became a part of this changing political landscape. These social movements more closely aligned their own views and approaches with those of the state – so much so that the Malaysian state recognized their roles in shaping politics, seeing these groups as representing the "embeddedness of Islamic concerns in the Malay community," and, concomitantly, as serving as "reliable indicators of the feelings, aspirations, and concerns of its Malay-Muslim majority electorate" (Mohd Kamal Hassan 2003: 98).

Meanwhile, as links between ABIM and UMNO deepened, IRC's more strident advocacy of the introduction of *shari'a* in Malaysia on the way to Islamic statehood led its members to see themselves as more naturally aligned with PAS, to which they started to gravitate in the 1980s. The relationship between PAS and activists from IRC, however, was short-lived. Relations were strained over an evident attempt by "extremists" in IRC to infiltrate PAS leadership with the objective of transforming the party into a vehicle for IRC's own political program. Brewing tensions boiled over at the 1987 PAS party elections when senior party leadership made a concerted effort to block IRC-affiliated candidates from winning senior positions in the party's youth council (Fadzillah Mohd Jamil 1988: 297). While some IRC leaders (for instance, Khalid Samad and Dzulkefly Ahmad) and members remained in PAS, others such as Wan Hasni and Rahim Ghouse shifted allegiances to UMNO. IRC itself would later morph into the more moderate organization, JIM.

5.3 Reformasi(s)

For the Tarbiyah movement in Indonesia, its foray into mainstream politics began with PK, which first contested as a political party in the 1998 elections. A failure to secure the necessary 2 percent of popular votes that it needed to qualify to run in the next election, in part because it was a newcomer and at the time an unknown entity, compelled PK to reevaluate its approach. The party was thereupon recast as "a populist, reform-oriented party" and renamed PKS (Noorhaidi Hasan 2009: 7–8). In its reconstituted form, PKS was able to improve on its predecessor's performance, in the process signaling its arrival as an increasingly consequential actor on the political scene.

At the 2004 Dewan Perwakilan Rakyat (House of Representatives) elections, PKS went on to win an impressive forty-five seats with a support base comprised primarily of younger, educated voters (Ahmad Ali Nurdin 2011: 334–337). Technically, this translated to 8.3 million votes for PKS candidates or 7.3 percent of the popular vote, not an inconsequential figure for a political party that was still somewhat new (Kompas 2005). Several factors accounted for its successful political campaign. First, its Islamo-democratic message of reform resonated in a climate defined by both political openness and growing religious piety; second, the cadreization structure of the Tarbiyah movement provided an effective grassroots political machinery that PKS had further developed with powerful effect since 1998; and finally, in addition to Islamization, its focus on the narrative of anti-corruption gave it wide appeal. It was on the back of this performance that PKS became the first Islamic party to be represented in a sitting government in Indonesia. Beyond its quantitative performance at the ballot box, what further distinguished PKS was the putative moderation of its Islamist agenda. As PKS legislator

Zulkieflimansyah explained, "from now on, we are going to talk more on issues pertaining to living standards and infrastructure, economic competitiveness and job opportunities. It is not our goal to set up an Islamic state or to implement syariah (*shari'a*) laws" (Salim Osman 2008). Indeed, it is interesting to note how, within the span of one electoral cycle, the political arm of an Islamic movement started campaigning on seemingly "secular" issues and even articulated slogans such as "Clean and Caring and Professional." Undergirding this was the ideological imperative to reconcile democracy with Islam. This was advocated by PKS voices such as Zulkifliemansyah and Hidayat Nur Wahid. In an opinion piece published in the *Jakarta Post*, Hidayat elaborated:

> The first consequence [of the effort to reconcile democracy with Islam] is egalitarianism and tolerance. A second consequence is the democratic principle of shura in Islam. Finally, a third consequence is that of moderation. According to Islam, humans are neither angels nor devils. They should not be materialistic or ascetic. Neither should they be on the far ends of individualism and collectivism. Islam rejects all extremes, whether in the form of consumerism or terrorism. At the same time, Islam encourages a democracy that can protect the weak and poor as well as supporting economic growth. (Hidayat Nur Wahid 2005)

At a national level, PKS has publicly accepted the secular nature of the Indonesian nation-state and its accompanying ideology, Pancasila, not to mention the 1945 Constitution and the democratic electoral system that has obtained since the end of the New Order. Yet, as a card-carrying Islamic political party, PKS has had in its own internal party discourse to align this commitment to the national ideology and constitution with its efforts to emphasize the importance of Islam as a source of its own identity and legitimacy (Noorhaidi Hasan 2009: 4). To that end, PKS has regularly asserted that the fundamental ideals of *tarbiyah*, to "establish an independent, caring and prosperous civil society that respects justice and to realize the principles of honest, clean transparent and responsible good governance," are in line with the Pancasila ideals of just humanity, true democracy, universal social justice, and the belief in God, as discussed in Section 3.2 (Noorhaidi Hasan 2009: 5). In so doing, PKS has demonstrated the veracity of arguments that, upon committing to the electoral process, Islamist parties tend to "normalize" or moderate themselves. In the case of PKS, this has manifested, among other ways, in its absorption of non-Muslims into its membership ranks; receptivity to coalition politics, including with secular parties; and support for candidates from other parties in local elections (Tanuwidjaja 2012).

At the same time, "normalization" and "moderation" should not be assumed to mean that PKS is prepared to abandon its original Islamist objectives. The reality is that the messages PKS articulates, not unlike those of PAS in Malaysia, can often be found to differ sharply, or at times may even be contradictory, depending on whether they are for public or internal consumption. In essence, PKS seized upon opportunities afforded by the opening up of political space in post-Suharto Indonesia that enabled it to negotiate a role in Indonesian society while adhering to the principles of their Tarbiyah roots. This is evident from its internal narrative explaining the essence of its political activism.

Emphasizing principles of *Shirka Iqtisadiyya* (ensuring economic strength and fair distribution) and *Fikra Ijtimaiyya* (commitment to resolving social problems) as advocated by Hassan al-Banna, PKS quickly evolved a narrative around the ideal of a "politics of service" and positioned itself as "an agent of the country's integration into liberal political and economic spaces" via its *tarbiyah* ideals of social responsibility, as well as widespread civil society initiatives such as Pos Keadilan Peduli Ummat (the Post for Care and Justice for the *Ummat*), Bulan Sabit Merah Indonesia (the Indonesian Red Crescent), and Pandu Keadilan (the Justice Scout program) (Noorhaidi Hasan 2009: 18). Another civil society or economic welfare initiative of PKS is the *Rumah Zakat*, which has helped the party "cultivate civil society organizations operating widely to reach society at the grassroots level," with the aim of providing consultancy services and advocacy for business incubation and labor associations (Noorhaidi Hasan 2009: 18). Through various channels, PKS has run a range of programs of economic empowerment by giving soft loans to more than 5,550 individuals and 912 independent small-enterprise groups, amounting to a circulation of about Rp.6.4 billion or approximately USD450,000 (Noorhaidi Hasan 2009: 19). According to the narrative PKS propagates, underscoring these social welfare initiatives is their self-declared drive to "liberate the masses and to make them active in the formulation [and] interpretation of Islam," eventually facilitating a return to the ideals of the Tarbiyah movement upon which PKS programs are predicated (Larrson 2011: 198).

It should be pointed out that PKS is not the only political party that draws from the wellsprings of the Islamic social movements that have been active in Indonesia. The National Awakening Party (Partai Kebangkitan Bangsa, or PKB), which straddles the conservative and pluralist ends of the spectrum of Islamic ideology in Indonesia, is closely linked to Indonesia's largest Muslim organization, NU, whose own traditionalist orientation has made it historically more tolerant of religious and cultural diversity. Similarly, the National Mandate Party (Partai Amanat Nasional, or PAN) has been the extension of Muhammadiyah, a modernist Islamic organization that is the second largest in the country. It is important to highlight, though, that Tarbiyah and its political party (PK, and later, PKS) function differently from the NU–PKB and Muhammadiyah–PAN combinations. This is because, unlike NU or Muhammadiyah, Tarbiyah lacks an overarching organizational identity, and by that token is not a registered entity bound by Indonesian laws and regulations the way Muhammadiyah and NU are.

The fact that emphatic public endorsement of democracy and pluralism in the ranks of PKS does not come at the expense of what they believe to be core Islamic beliefs and practices has been made more clear by the party's stand on a range of issues, such as the Anti-Pornography Bill, for which the party led the charge in 2008 to ensure a formulation that was expansive in its interpretation of what passes for pornography. Also, during the 2017 gubernatorial elections in Jakarta, Islamic social movements mobilized in opposition to the ethnic-Chinese Christian candidate, Basuki Tjahaja Purnama or Ahok, on the grounds that he had allegedly made blasphemous remarks. While the case against Ahok was controversial on a number of counts (some have argued that the allegedly blasphemous remarks were taken out of context, while others suggested that entrenched political interests opposed to Ahok had manipulated the Islamic movements that mobilized to protest his candidature), the point to stress for present purposes is that opportunists and political entrepreneurs deliberately spun a narrative against Ahok around issues of "blasphemy" and "defending the (Islamic) faith," with the intent of mobilizing a mass base – in this case, Islamists – against a particular candidate, and it was this narrative that gained currency among large segments of the Tarbiyah community that rallied under the PKS banner (Sumanto Al Qurtuby 2018).

Just as the Indonesian Reformasi catalyzed Tarbiyah, the Malaysian Reformasi, which occurred at the same time as its Indonesian counterpart, transformed Dakwah by opening up further opportunities for political involvement. Indeed, the Islamic resurgence in Malaysia moved from a *dakwah*-based to a politically based movement with the emergence of the Anwar-led Reformasi movement, when the former deputy prime minister's expulsion from the UMNO-led government resulted in the formation of an opposition movement that featured Islamic and Islamist groups prominently. Removed from power ostensibly for alleged corruption and sexual offences, Anwar launched a diatribe against the Mahathir-led government for his dismissal from office and subsequent trial, incarceration, and abuse suffered while in detention. This, in turn, impelled mobilization by diverse Muslim civil society groups, many of whom enjoyed strong relationships with Anwar traceable to his days as a Dakwah activist, for greater justice and accountability. This mobilization gave rise to the nationwide reform movement that bore some semblance to what was unfolding in Indonesia. A notable feature of this social movement mobilization was the influx of activists into political parties to "make a real difference."[12]

Not surprisingly, the Islamist opposition, PAS, became a major beneficiary. As a political party, PAS formed for the explicit purpose of achieving political power, albeit with religion as its primary referent. As the party leadership itself has explained:

> Implementing the laws of Allah in the form of ibadah [worship] such as fasting, praying, paying zakat, performing pilgrimage and so on is relatively easy but to implement other laws of Allah such as laws, economic, political, and social systems and so on is not easy, unless by establishing an Islamic government. Based on this fact, it is a reality that power is the main condition in implementing the laws of Allah. For this reason, the struggle for governing power, to PAS, is a must for every Muslim. And it is this governing power that is called political power. It is such political power that has been the struggle for PAS for so long. Political power is a means of implementing the laws of Allah. The laws of Islam cannot be implemented automatically unless through a governing institution. Only the government that strives for the laws of Islam can guarantee implementation of the laws of Allah. It is based on this fact that PAS has chosen the struggle through a political party which is based on Islam as a policy for Islamic rule. Therefore, what PAS strives for must be supported by society, especially by Muslims in this country. (PAS Pusat undated: 6–7)

This premise represented PAS's political objective – in fact, it captured the logic of the party's very existence.

As an *"ulama* party" since the introduction of clerical leadership in 1983, PAS had started to change its complexion by the late 1980s, initially with the gradual, but short-lived influx of IRC activists mentioned previously. Reformasi offered PAS a second attempt to accommodate Islamic social movement actors, as the party was positioned to profit from a surge in membership from among civil society activists. These activists, mainly from ABIM and JIM, but also from some other groups, infused a stronger sense of purpose into the Islamist opposition party and formed the backbone of what observers would later somewhat inaccurately describe as the "professional" or "progressive" camp within the party. Even with this changing profile, the party strove to maintain the essence of its objectives. On the question of whether they would eschew the objective of the creation of an Islamic state in Malaysia, a highly ranked member of the "professional" camp was elusive, responding that "our priority at the moment is not to create an Islamic state but to Islamize society from

---

[12] Interview with a former ABIM member, August 22, 2020.

below. The creation of an Islamic state will come naturally once we can achieve that."[13] The ambiguity and elusiveness in this response provides insight into a tension that had crept into the party by way of the influence that "progressives" were beginning to enjoy: whereas the traditional *ulama* leadership of PAS were emphatic about the establishment of an Islamic state by fiat, which explains persistent efforts on their part to articulate an Islamic state "policy" to guide their politics, social movement activists who flocked to the party during the height of Reformasi retained their belief in mobilization from below by way of *dakwah*.

In the event, many of these social activists would eventually leave PAS in 2015 after they were defeated in party elections that year. At that point, they were engaged in an acrimonious struggle over whether the future of the party lay with the multi-ethnic reformist coalition, Pakatan Harapan, or with ethnona-tionalist UMNO, which itself was becoming an advocate of an exclusivist brand of Islamism laced with racist overtones. These Islamist activists would go on to form Parti Amanah Negara, positioning themselves as reformist Islamic democrats.

PAS was not the only beneficiary of the process of political socialization that Malaysian Islamic social movements underwent during the Reformasi years. At the height of Reformasi, Fadzil Noor, then president of PAS and a close compatriot of Anwar from their ABIM days, spearheaded efforts to form Gerak, a coalition of opposition political parties and Muslim and non-Muslim non-governmental organizations that mobilized around the cause célèbre of Anwar's freedom. Activists from ABIM and JIM who had followed Anwar into UMNO through the 1980s and 1990s broke ranks with the incumbent regime and became its harshest critics as they flocked to the opposition. The surge was such that in the foment building up to the 1999 general election, a senior opposition politician expressed concern that "while it is great to see the upsurge of support and membership increase, I am concerned that we [the opposition political parties] are thinning out the Islamic NGOs by relying on their activists. What if we don't win? What would become of these NGOs and their struggle?"[14] Reformasi also witnessed the coalescing of groups into another social movement, KeAdilan, which eventually evolved into Parti Keadilan Nasional or PKN, and eventually into Parti Keadilan Rakyat or PKR, the People's Justice Party, in April 1999. PKR would become the phalanx for the Reformasi movement and the vehicle for Anwar's continued political

---

[13] Interview, Kuala Lumpur, February 17, 2013.

[14] This quote is taken from my research in 1999, during the buildup to the general election. In the event, the Malaysian opposition failed to unseat the UMNO-led Barisan Nasional, but not without first inflicting a 10 percent swing in the popular vote away from the incumbent.

engagement. Long on zeal and idealism but (at the time) short on organizational capacity, PKR relied on PAS as well as its (and Anwar's) allies from the Dakwah movement to mobilize, organize, and contest elections.

Although PAS and PKR failed to unseat the ruling coalition at the 1999 election, unbeknown to the actors involved in the generation-defining event of that era, the struggle they had begun would last two decades, culminating in the toppling of the UMNO-led government in 2018. During this time, a vibrant landscape of Islamic social activism would take shape as a host of Islamic and Islamist organizations, drawing inspiration from the legacy of Dakwah, mobilized to influence and shape Islamic discourse and politics in Malaysia.

6 Conclusions

The role that Islam plays as an agent of social and political change has emerged over the last two decades as a key theme in the study of politics in Indonesia and Malaysia. Taking the Islamic revival of the late 1960s and early 1970s as its chronological point of entry, this Element has attempted an assessment of Islamism in the context of these two Muslim-majority Southeast Asian societies from the vantage point of its roots in Islamic social movements. Focusing attention on two of the most consequential mass-based Islamic social movements in Southeast Asia – the Tarbiyah movement in Indonesia and Dakwah in Malaysia – the preceding analysis has identified the key Islamist signifiers these movements have articulated as their intellectual and ideational foundations, as well as how they have evolved organizationally in their efforts to institutionalize these signifiers towards the end of transforming politics and society. As a case in point, *shari'a* is stock in trade for Islamists, hardwired into their agenda as a political signifier. Consequently, it should be no surprise that in both Indonesia and Malaysia, Islamist political parties have placed *shari'a* at the forefront of their respective national programs, attempting to align it with democratic principles. That said, the shari'aization effort is far more advanced in Malaysia, especially given the prerogative of states to regulate matters pertaining to religion under the Malaysian federal system of government.

Given the argument this study offers, that Islamist social movements have been instrumental in shaping and transforming narratives and expressions of Islamism in the political sphere, it is hardly unexpected to find that Islamic social movements have been active in advocating for *shari'a*; not only that, but they have been deeply engaged in shaping the discourses surrounding it, as well. At the height of its popularity in the 1970s, ABIM was recognized as one of the most ardent advocates of *shari'a* (Abu Bakar 1981: 1045). The same can be said of the Tarbiyah movement, particularly after it became more visible in the mid-1980s.

This discourse is itself nuanced, as advocates relate the importance of *shari'a* not so much to the brusque objective of the creation of an Islamic state, but more to the shaping Muslim outlooks and attitudes more generally.

Not only were Islamist signifiers and their underlying logics consequential, so, too, were these movements' methods of organization and mobilization. Specifically, this dimension includes key leadership personalities and the roles they have played in framing discourses and shaping narratives, as well as the networks that Islamic movements have created – particularly in the spheres of knowledge production and education – and that have, in turn, served as vehicles through which ideas have been disseminated and internalized. On this score, the role of transnational networks has been especially important, particularly how heavily Tarbiyah in Indonesia and Dakwah groups in Malaysia borrowed from Ikhwanul Muslimin's organizational model, along with recruitment and indoc-trination strategies centered on education institutions and study groups, in order to organize and mobilize to effect change. At a deeper level, the role of the Ikhwanul Muslimin suggests the influence of ideas emanating from the heart-land of the Islamic world, which have permeated into and shaped the thinking of Southeast Asian Islamic intellectuals over time, has been instrumental to the emergence of an activist and engaged Islamist social movement landscape. Southeast Asian scholars and students internalized these ideas during their sojourns abroad or encounters locally with Ikhwan intellectuals. Tarbiyah and Dakwah introduced and assimilated these ideas into the local context, negotiat-ing with prevailing social and political climates in Indonesia and Malaysia.

At the same time, while there is a tendency among Southeast Asian Muslims to genuflect in the direction of the Islamic heartland in the Middle East – not just literally in terms of the direction of prayer but also figuratively in terms of what is received as "authentic" Islam – the transmission of knowledge and experience is not necessarily unidirectional. To be sure, it remains the case that when Islamism first sunk roots in Southeast Asia, its adherents drew lessons on how to effect social and political change predicated on religious identity from the experiences of social movements and political parties in the Middle East. For instance, in the early days of Dakwah, Islamic institutions in Malaysia, such as Kelang Islamic College, employed academics from Al-Azhar University, a center of Ikhwanul Muslimin activism. However, in recent times we see evidence of some degree of the reverse happening: Islamism in Southeast Asia appears to be exercising some measure of influence on the Islamic heart-land. Encouraging that process is the fact that, in Southeast Asia, political parties such as PKS in Indonesia and PAS in Malaysia have accumulated considerable experience in government by virtue of their absorption – through coalition building – into government administrations. Malaysia's PAS has also had long-standing experience running state administrations in their bastions in northern Malaysia, so much so that, upon coming to power on the back of the Arab Spring, Ikhwan politicians had in fact reached out to these Southeast Asian counterparts to seek advice on governance.

A further point about the Ikhwanul Muslimin and its influence in among Indonesian and Malaysian Islamists bears noting. While the movement has a strong sense of identity, organizational culture, and purpose, it is by no means a uniform, monolithic movement. A detailed analysis of the different ideological and political shades within the Ikhwan movement is beyond the scope of this study. Suffice to say that the numerous chapters of the Ikhwan found in Egypt, Syria, Tunisia, Libya, and Morocco suggest that diverse outlooks in fact prevail under the broad umbrella of the movement. Concomitantly, it should not be a surprise to find similar diversity within the Tarbiyah or Dakwah movements and their political offshoots. Indeed, as we have seen, this has been precisely the case. In the example of Tarbiyah and its relationship with PKS, the intimate links between them have not precluded discernible divergences as well. Masdar Hilmy explains:

> Since the two organizations operate in different arenas, the one political and the other social, and are governed under different regulations, inevitably they have developed different sets of rules and procedures that sometimes are not compatible with each other: JT [Jemaah Tarbiyah, or the Tarbiyah movement] as a social religious organization operates under the principles of personal ethics and piety, while PKS engages in political power struggles and mostly operates under the principles of programmatic achievements and accountability. Consequently, the two often clash with each other. (Masdar Hilmy 2009: 257–258).

Much in the same vein, tensions have also been evident between Dakwah organizations in Malaysia, such as ABIM and IRC, and the mainstream Islamist parties, UMNO and PAS.

At this juncture, it would be useful to consider the degree of cooperation – or apparent lack thereof – between Indonesian and Malaysian movements. To be sure, there is evidence of, if not cooperation, then at least overlap and awareness. For instance, Anwar Ibrahim was known to have enjoyed close personal ties with Mohamad Natsir, and he also spent time in Indonesia with the DDII during his days as an ABIM activist. Be that as it may, the dearth of cross-pollination between Indonesian and Malaysian social movements and Islamist political parties has been striking, especially given intuitive assumptions that ethnocultural and linguistic affinity, as well as geographic proximity, would foster cooperation. As the preceding discussion has shown, the fundamentally different trajectories that Islamism has traversed in these two countries accounts in no small measure for this lack.

Three observations shed light on this divergence. First, we find a major point of departure in how Tarbiyah and Dakwah have blended into the landscape of mainstream politics in their respective countries. In Indonesia, politicians with a Tarbiyah background are almost all to be found in PKS, given the robust cadreization programs that the Islamist social movement introduced at its inception and maintained through the transition into mainstream politics. In Malaysia, however, Dakwah activists-turned-politicians can be found across the spectrum of political parties – in UMNO, PAS, Amanah, and PKR – indicating a more diffused influence.

Second, notwithstanding the existence of progressive voices within its camp, Islamist political activism in Malaysia has, in the main, taken a narrow and exclusivist turn. Exemplifying (and personifying) this is the role that Hadi Awang, the former Dakwah activist who is currently president and chief ideologue of PAS, has assumed. Under his leadership, PAS has pressed ahead with an Islamization agenda with the objective of implementing the entire counsel of Islamic law, including a controversial penal code. A host of vocal Islamist civil society groups have supported PAS in this endeavor, linking the implementation of Islamic law and creation of an Islamic state with an assertion of Islamic identity and Malay rights. Because of the perceived existential nature of the enterprise, it has also won endorsement – mostly tacit, but at times explicit – from UMNO, which remains the dominant Malay-Muslim political party. On the other hand, in the case of Indonesia, PKS has, at least on the surface, resisted pressure to pursue a more robust Islamist agenda. Moreover, while conservative religious forces actively engage in debates over social issues, there has been no concerted effort to promote the Islamic state as a signal political objective.

Third, the role of the state – and the nature of its relationship with the Islamist social movements under consideration here – has not been inconsequential. Notwithstanding something of a correlation between the opening of political space and an upsurge in Islamist activism, the fact is that, in Malaysia, the state has since the 1970s played an instrumental role in gradually creating the enabling environment that allowed Islamist activism to thrive. In Indonesia, however, suppression at the hands of the New Order state enervated Islamism and forced it underground, where it was in part sustained by the Tarbiyah movement. Equally salient is the fact that, apart from a brief period immediately after the fall of President Suharto, when Pancasila came under heavy scrutiny for its connection with the New Order regime, its role and acceptance as an expression of national cohesion has also moderated the appeal of Islamism in ways that have been absent from Malaysian discourse on Islam, Islamism, and national identity.

All told, while scholars of both Indonesia and Malaysia have recognized that Islam has grown in prominence and influence, shaping politics and society in profound ways, this phenomenon did not happen overnight. Indeed, while ideas and institutions undoubtedly played important roles for all the reasons enumerated above, so, too, has the larger social and political landscape in which they operate. Crucially, this landscape offered up what social movement theorists term "political opportunities," through which key Islamist social movements have shaped political activism and mobilized for change. For reasons elaborated here, the governments in both Indonesia and Malaysia eventually accommodated Islamic resurgence instead of suppressing it. This allowed Tarbiyah and Dakwah, building on their model of grassroots-based collective action, to penetrate more deeply and influence the pulse of Muslim society in Indonesia and Malaysia, projecting their ideals not just as abstract religious, political, or social ideas, but as lived experience. Ultimately then, a full understanding of the appeal of Islamism in Indonesia and Malaysia today requires appreciation of the social movements with which many Islamist causes have been imbricated. With deeply embedded roots in civil and political activism, these Islamist social movements – and their political avatars – have been able to shape broader political discourse and will in all likelihood continue to do so for the foreseeable future.

References

Abd. Hadi Borham (2018). "Media Baharu dan Impak Terhadap Dakwah," *Sains Humanika* 10(3/4): 51–60.

Abdul Hadi Awang (1985). *Muqadimmah Aqidah Muslimin*. Petaling Jaya: Sarjana Media.

Ahmad Ali Nurdin (2011). "PKS' Democratic Experience in Recruiting Members and Leaders," *Al-Jāmi'ah* 49(2): 329–360.

Ahmad Fauzi Abdul Hamid (2003). "The Maturation of Dakwah in Malaysia: Divergence and Convergence in the Methods of Islamic Movements in the 1980s," *Jurnal IKIM* 11(2), July/December: 59–97.

Ahmad Fauzi Abdul Hamid (2009). "Transnational Islam in Malaysia," in *Transnational Islam in South and Southeast Asia*, eds. Peter Mandaville et al. Washington, DC: National Bureau of Asian Research, pp. 141–165.

Ahmad Lutfi Othman (1992). *Selepas Mahathir Peluang PAS*. Kuala Lumpur: Penerbitan Pemuda.

Ahmad Norma Permata (2016). "A Study on the Internal Dynamics of the Prosperous Justic Party and Jamaah Tarbiyah," in *Islam, Politics, and Change: The Indonesian Experience After the Fall of Suharto*, eds. Kees van Dijk and Nico J. G. Kaptein. Leiden: Leiden University Press, pp. 29–77.

Ai Fatimah Nur Fuad (2017). "Islamism and Dakwah in Late Modern Indonesia: Official Discourses and Lived Experiences of Leaders and Members of the Tarbiyah Movement." PhD dissertation, University of Leeds.

Ai Fatimah Nur Fuad (2020). "Kajian Literatur tentang Perkembangan Historis dan Transformasi Dakwah Gerakan Tarbiyah di Indonesia," *Jurnal Lektur Keagamaan* 17(2), February: 349–382.

Aini Maznina A. Manaf (2018). "Dakwah Melalui Media Baharu Di Malaysia: Peluang Atau Cabaran?" *Al-Hikmah* 10(1): 119–128.

Ali Abdul Halim Mahmud (2004). *Perangkat-Perangkat Tarbiyah Ikhwanul Muslimin*, trans. Wahid Ahmadi et al. Solo: Intermedia.

Anderson, Jon W. (2000). "New Media in the Muslim World: The Emerging Public Sphere," *ISIM Newsletter* 5(1): 39.

Anria, Santiago (2019). *When Movements Become Parties: The Bolivian MAS in Comparative Perspective*. Cambridge: Cambridge University Press.

Anwar Ibrahim (1989). *Menangani Perubahan*. Kuala Lumpur: Berita Publishing.

Astro Awani (2014). "ABIM Calls on Dr. Mahathir to Retract Statement on Hudud Law," *Astro Awani*, April 22. http://english.astroawani.com/malaysia-news/abim-calls-dr-mahathir-retract-statement-hudud-law-34439.

Azmil Tayeb (2018). *Islamic Education in Indonesia and Malaysia: Shaping Minds, Saving Souls*. London: Routledge.

Baczko, Adam, Gilles Dorronsoro, and Arthur Quesnay (2018). *Civil War in Syria*. Cambridge: Cambridge University Press.

Bahtiar Effendy (2003). *Islam and the State in Indonesia*. Singapore: ISEAS.

Barendregt, Bart (2008). "Sex, Cannibals, and the Language of Cool: Indonesian Tales of the Phone and Modernity," *The Information Society* 24(3): 160–170.

Bayat, Asef (2002). "Activism and Social Development in the Middle East," *International Journal of Middle East Studies* 34(1): 1–28.

Bayat, Asef (2007). *Making Islam Democratic: Social Movements and the Post-Islamist Turn*. Palo Alto, CA: Stanford University Press.

Bennet, W. Lance (2005). "Social Movements beyond Borders: Organization, Communication, and Political Capacity in Two Eras of Transnational Activism," in *Transnational Protest and Global Activism*, eds. Donatella della Porta and Sidney Tarrow. Lanham, MD: Rowman & Littlefield, pp. 203–226.

Brown, Leon Carl (2000). *Religion and State: The Muslim Approach to Politics*. New York: Columbia University Press.

Bubalo, Anthony and Greg Fealy (2005). *Joining the Caravan? The Middle East, Islamism and Indonesia*. Double Day, NSW: Longueville Media.

Buechler, Steven M. (1995). "New Social Movement Theories," *The Sociological Quarterly* 36(3): 441–464.

Buehler, Michael (2008). "The Rise of Shari'a By-Laws in Indonesian Districts: An Indication for Changing Patterns of Power Accumulation and Political Corruption," *South East Asia Research* 16(2): 255–285.

Bunt, Gary R. (2003). *Islam in the Digital Age: E-jihad, Online Fatwas and Cyber Islamic Environments*. London: Pluto Press.

Bunt, Gary R. (2009). *iMuslims: Rewiring the House of Islam*. London: Hurst.

Cammett, Melani and Pauline Jones Luong (2014). "Is There an Islamist Political Advantage?" *Annual Review of Political Science* 17: 187–206.

Chernov-Hwang, Julie (2009). *Peaceful Islamist Mobilisation in the Muslim World*. New York: Palgrave Macmillan.

Claessen, Eric A. (2010). *Stalemate: An Anatomy of Conflicts Between Democracies, Islamists, and Muslim Autocrats*. Santa Barbara, CA: Praeger.

Crouch, Harold (1996). *Government and Politics in Malaysia*. Ithaca, NY: Cornell University Press.

Danahar, Paul (2013). *The New Middle East: The World After the Arab Spring*. New York: Bloomsbury Press.

De Nardis, Fabio (2020). *Understanding Politics and Society.* London: Palgrave Macmillan.

Diani, Mario (1992). "The Concept of a Social Movement," *The Sociological Review* 40(1): 1–25.

Diani, Mario (2003). "Introduction," in *Social Movements and Networks: Relational Approaches to Collective Action*, eds. Mario Diani and Douglas McAdam. New York: Oxford University Press, pp. 1–20.

Diani, Mario (2013). "Networks and Social Movements," in *The Wiley-Blackwell Encyclopaedia of Social and Political Movements*, eds. David A. Snow, Donatella della Porta, Bert Klandermans, and Doug McAdam. Malden, MA: Wiley-Blackwell, pp. 835–840.

Earl, Jennifer and Katrina Kimport (2011). *Digitally Enabled Social Change: Activism in the Internet Age.* Cambridge, MA: MIT Press.

Esposito, John L., Yvonne Yazbeck Haddad, Kathleen Moore, David Sawan, and John O. Voll (1991). *The Contemporary Islamic Revival: A Critical Survey and Bibliography.* Westport, CT: Greenwood Press.

Fadzillah Mohd. Jamil (1988). "The Reawakening of Islamic Consciousness in Malaysia: 1970–1987." PhD dissertation, University of Edinburgh.

Fahlesa Munabari (2017). "Reconciling Sharia with 'Negara Kesatuan Republik Indonesia': The Ideology and Framing Strategies of the Indonesian Forum of Islamic Society (FUI)," *International Area Studies Review* 20(3): 242–263.

Faisal Ismail (2011). "The Nahdlatul Ulama: Its Early History and Contribution to the Establishment of Indonesian State," *Journal of Indonesian Islam* 5(2): 247–282.

Fealy, Greg and Virginia Hooker (eds.) (2006). *Voices of Islam in Southeast Asia: A Contemporary Sourcebook.* Singapore: Institute of Southeast Asian Studies.

Febrian Taufik Saleh (2015). "Manhaj Tarbiyah dalam Pendidikan Politik PKS," *Salam* 19(1): 1–18.

Fouad Ajami (1981). *The Arab Predicament: Arab Political Thought and Practice since 1967.* Cambridge: Cambridge University Press.

Freeman, Karen Sabina (2013). "News Consumption Behavior of Young Adults in Malaysia," *International Journal of Social Science and Humanity* 3(2), March: 121–124.

Grand, Stephen R. (2014). *Understanding Tahrir Square.* Washington, DC: Brookings Institution Press.

Hafez Ghanem (2016). *The Arab Spring: Five Years Later.* Washington, DC: Brookings Institution Press.

Halliday, Fred (2005). *The Middle East in International Relations: Power, Politics, and Ideology*. Cambridge: Cambridge University Press.

Halpern, Manfred (1963). *The Politics of Social Change in the Middle East and North Africa*. Princeton, NJ: Princeton University Press.

Hamid Dabashi (2012). *The Arab Spring: The End of Postcolonialism*. London: Zed Books.

Hassan Al-Banna (2001). *Risalah Pergerakan 2*. Solo: Intermedia.

Hassan Omar (2017). "Apa Beza ABIM dengan IRC?" *Lebai Haji Hassan Omar*, June. https://hajihassanomar.blogspot.com/2017/06/apa-beza-abim-dengan-irc.html.

Hefner, Robert W. (2009). "Islamic Schools, Social Movements, and Democracy in Indonesia," in *Making Modern Muslims: The Politics of Islamic Education in Southeast Asia*, ed. Robert W. Hefner. Honolulu: University of Hawaii Press, pp. 55–105.

Hew, Wai Weng (2017). "Malay Politics Meets Islamic Activism in Malaysia's Act 355," *ISEAS Perspectives*, April 3.

Hidayat Nur Wahid (2005). "Islam, Democracy, and Politics in Indonesia," *Jakarta Post*, September 9.

Hidayatullah (2000). "Profesional dari Mujahid Kampus," April.

Hitti, Philips K. (1949). *History of the Arabs*. London: Macmillan and Co.

Irfun Teguh (2018). "Rahmat Abdullah: Lambang Spiritualisme Gerakan Dakwah Tarbiyah," *Tirto.id*, June 8. https://tirto.id/rahmat-abdullah-lambang-spiritualisme-gerakan-dakwah-tarbiyah-cKYn.

Irwandani (2016). "Potensi Media Sosial dalam Mempopulerkan Konten Sains Islam," *Tadris: Jurnal Keguruan dan Ilmu Tarbiyah* 1(2): 173–177.

Kahin, Audrey (ed.) (1985). *Regional Dynamics of the Indonesian Revolution*. Honolulu: University of Hawaii Press.

Kahin, Audrey R. (2012). *Islam, Nationalism and Democracy: A Political Biography of Mohammad Natsir*. Singapore: NUS Press.

Kahin, George McTurnan (1952). *Nationalism and Revolution in Indonesia*. Ithaca, NY: Cornell University Press.

Kementerian Agama RI (2019/2020). "Data Statistik Pendidikan Islam," *EMIS Dashboard*, 2019/2020. http://emispendis.kemenag.go.id/dashboard/?content=data-statistik.

Kepel, Gilles (2002). *Jihad: The Trail of Political Islam*. Cambridge, MA: Harvard University Press.

Khalil Al-Anani (2016). *Inside the Muslim Brotherhood: Religion, Identity, and Politics*. Oxford: Oxford University Press.

Khatib, Line (2012). *Islamic Revivalism in Syria: The Rise and Fall of Ba'ath Secularism*. London: Routledge.

Kitschelt, Herbert P. (2006). "Movement Parties," in *Handbook of Party Politics*, eds. Richard S. Katz and William J. Crotty. London: Sage Publications, pp. 278–290.

Kompas (2005). "Jajak Pendapat 'Kompas': PKS, Menuai Buah Konsistensi," *Kompas*, June 25.

Kompasiana (2018). "Islam, Indonesia, dan Generasi Milenial," *Kompasiana*, February 4. www.kompasiana.com/muhammadsultana/5a49eaaef133447eec6b 9652/islam-indonesia-dan-generasi-millennials.

Koopmans, Ruud (2004). "Political Opportunity Structure: Some Splitting to Balance the Lumping," in *Rethinking Social Movements*, eds. Jeff Goodwin and James M. Jasper. Lanham MD: Rowman & Littlefield, pp. 61–74.

Kramer, Elisabeth (2014). "A Fall from Grace? 'Beef-gate' and the Case of Indonesia's Prosperous Justice Party," *Asian Politics and Policy* 6(4): 555–576.

Kuru, Ahmet T. (2019). *Islam, Authoritarianism, and Underdevelopment: A Global and Historical Comparison*. Cambridge: Cambridge University Press.

Lapidus, Ira M. (1997). "Islamic Revival and Modernity: The Contemporary Movements and the Historical Paradigms," *Journal of the Economic and Social History of the Orient* 40(4): 444–460.

Larrson, Goran (2011). *Muslims and the New Media: Historical and Contemporary Debates*. London: Ashgate.

Liow, Joseph Chinyong (2009). *Piety and Politics: Islamism in Contemporary Malaysia*. New York: Oxford University Press.

Liow, Joseph Chinyong (2016). *Religion and Nationalism in Southeast Asia*. Cambridge: Cambridge University Press.

Lukman Hakiem and Tansil Linrung (1997). *Menunaikan Panggilan Risalah: Dokumentasi Perjalan 30 Tahun DDII*. Jakarta: DDII.

Mandaville, Peter (2001). *Transnational Muslim Politics: Reimagining the Umma*. London: Routledge.

Mandaville, Peter (2014). *Islam and Politics*, 2nd ed. London: Routledge.

Masdar Hilmy (2009). *Islamism and Democracy in Indonesia: Piety and Pragmatism*. Singapore: ISEAS.

Maszlee Malik and Hamidah Mat (2014). "Pious Approach to Development: Social Capital and Pertubuhan Jemaah Islah Malaysia (JIM)," *World Journal of Islamic History and Civilization* 4(3): 107–118.

McAdam, Doug, Sidney G. Tarrow, and Charles Tilly (2001). *Dynamics of Contention*. Cambridge: Cambridge University Press.

Mecham, Quinn and Julie Chernov-Hwang (eds.) (2014). *Islamist Parties and Political Normalization in the Muslim World*. Philadelphia: University of Pennsylvania Press.

Mohamad Abu Bakar (1981). "Islamic Revivalism and the Political Process in Malaysia," *Asian Survey* 21(10): 1040–1059.

Mohamed Imran Mohamed Taib (2012). "Neofundamentalist Thought, Dakwah and Religious Pluralism Among Muslims in Singapore," *International Sociological Association (ISA) e-Symposium for Sociology* 2(3). https://dialogosphere.wordpress.com/2016/03/02/neofundamentalist-thought-dakwah-and-religious-pluralism-among-muslims-in-singapore/.

Mohamed Nawab Mohamed Osman and Saleena Saleem (2016). "The Impact of Islamic Civil Society Organisations on Malaysian Islam and Politics," *RSIS Malaysia Update*, April 21.

Mohammad Ayoob (2007). *The Many Faces of Political Islam: Religion and Politics in the Muslim World*. Ann Arbor: University of Michigan Press.

Mohd Anuar Tahir (1993). *Pendirian Politik ABIM*. Petaling Jaya: Angkatan Belia Islam Malaysia.

Mohd Kamal Hassan (1997). "Islamic Studies in Contemporary Southeast Asia: Some Observations," in *Islamic Studies in ASEAN: Presentations of an International Seminar*. Pattani: Prince of Songkla University, pp. 487–488.

Mohd Kamal Hassan (2003). "The Influence of Mawdudi's Thought on Muslims in Southeast Asia: A Brief Survey," *The Muslim World* 93(3/4): 429–464.

Muhammad Sa'id (2003). "Tarbiyah Suatu Kemestian," in *Tarbiyah Berkelanjutan*, ed. Rahmat Abdullah and Somo Arifianto. Jakarta: Pustaka Tarbiatuna, pp. 45–52.

Muhammad Syahban Siddiq, Hafied Cangara, and A. Alimuddin Unde (2011). "Pemanfaatan Jaringan Komunikasi dalam Rekrutmen Kader Partai Keadilan Sejahtera Sulawesi Selatan," *Jurnal Komunikasi KAREBA* 1(4), October–December: 423–433.

Mustaqim Pabbajah, Hasse Jubba, Ratri Nurina Widyanti, Taufiq Pabbajah, and S. Iribaram (2019). "Internet of Religion: Islam and New Media Construction of Religious Movements in Indonesia," *Proceedings of the 19th Annual International Conference on Islamic Studies*, October 1–4, Jakarta, Indonesia: 1–9.

Nepstad, Sharon Erickson and Bob Clifford (2006). "When Do Leaders Matter? Hypotheses on Leadership Dynamics in Social Movements," *Mobilization* 11(1): 1–22.

Nielsen, Richard A. (2016). "The Changing Face of Islamic Authority in the Middle East," *Middle East Brief* 99: 3.

Nilan, Pam and Michelle Mansfield (2014). "Youth Culture and Islam in Indonesia," *Wacana* 15(1): 1–18.

Nisa, Eva F. (2018). "Social Media and the Birth of an Islamic Social Movement: ODOJ (One Day One Juz) in Contemporary Indonesia," *Indonesia and the Malay World* 46(134): 24–43.

Noor Firman (2015). *Perpecahan & Soliditas, Partai Islam Di Indonesia: Kasus PKB dan PKS Di Dekade Awal Reformasi*. Jakarta: Lembaga Ilmu Pengetahuan Indonesia.

Noorhaidi Hasan (2007). "The Salafi Movement in Indonesia: Transnational Dynamics and Local Development," *Comparative Studies of South Asia, Africa and the Middle East* 27(1): 83–94.

Noorhaidi Hasan (2009). "Islamist Party, Electoral Politics, and Da'wa Mobilization among Youth: The Prosperous Justice Party (PKS) in Indonesia," *RSIS Working Paper* 184, October.

NU Online (2020a). "Ketua PBNU: Indonesia Sudah Sesuai Syariat Islam," *NU Online*, February 24. www.nu.or.id/post/read/117095/ketua-pbnu–indonesia-sudah-sesuai-syariat-islam.

NU Online (2020b). "NU Menegaskan Hubungan Pancasila dengan Islam," *NU Online*, July 5. www.nu.or.id/post/read/116613/nu-menegaskan-hubungan-pancasila-dengan-islam.

Nurdin Rusli (2013). "Spiritualising New Media: The Use of Social Media for Da'wah Purposes within Indonesian Muslim Scholars," *Jurnal Komunikasi Islam* 3(1): 1–21.

Öniş, Ziyah (2006). "The Political Economy of Turkey's Justice and Development Party," in *The Emergence of a New Turkey: Islam, Democracy, and the Emergence of the AK Parti*, ed. Hakan Yavuz. Salt Lake City: University of Utah Press, pp. 207–234.

Osman Bakar (1993). "Implikasi Gerakan Dakwah ke atas Sistem Pendidikan Negara kini," in *Gerakan Dakwah dan Orde Islam di Malaysia: Strategi Masa Depan*, ed. ABIM. Petaling Jaya: ABIM, pp. 45–52.

PAS Pusat, Jabatan Penerangan (undated). *Memahami dan Mengenali Pejuangan Parti Islam SeMalaysia (PAS)*. Kuala Lumpur: PAS Pusat.

Pernau, Margarit (2003). "The Delhi Urdu Akhbar between Persian Akhbarat and English Newspapers," *The Annual of Urdu Studies* 18: 105–131.

Prayogi, Arditya (2019). "Masuk dan Perkembangannya Gerakan Tarbiyah, Studi Kasus: Gerakan Dakwa Kampus di Kampus Institut Teknologi bandung (ITB) 1983–1998," *Sindang: Jurnal Pendidikan Sejarah dan Kajian Sejarah* 1(1): 45–57.

Republika (2012). "Muhammadiyah: Pancasila Sesuai dengan Nilai Islam," *Republika*, June 24.

Republika (2017). "Pertumbuhan Pesantren di Indonesia Dinilai Menakjubkan," *Republika*, November 30.

Republika (2019). "DDII: Istilah Syariah Kerap Disalahpahami," *Republika*, July 17.

Roald, Anne Sofie (1994). *Tarbiya: Education and Politics in Islamic Movements in Jordan and Malaysia*. Lund: Religionshistoriska Avdelningen, Lunds Universitet.

Roff, William R. (1967). *The Origins of Malay Nationalism*. New Haven, CT: Yale University Press.

Roff, William R. (1998). "Patterns of Islamization in Malaysia, 1980s to 1990s: Exemplars, Institutions, and Vectors," *Journal of Islamic Studies* 9(2), July: 210–228.

Roy, Olivier (1998). *The Failure of Political Islam*. Cambridge, MA: Harvard University Press.

Rupp, Leila J. and Verta Taylor (1987). *Survival in the Doldrums: The American Women's Rights Movement, 1945 to the 1960s*. New York: Oxford University Press.

Saari Sungib (1994). *Aktivisme JIM 1993–1995*. Kuala Lumpur: Jamaah Islah Malaysia.

Saari Sungib (1995). *Menggerak Gagasan 1995–2000: Bersama Menggaris Agenda Ummah*. Kuala Lumpur: Pertubuhan Jamaah Islah Malaysia.

Saliha Hassan (2003). "Islamic Non-governmental Organisations," in *Social Movements in Malaysia: From Moral Communities to NGOs*, eds. Meredith L. Weiss and Saliha Hassan. London: Routledge Curzon, 2003, pp. 97–114.

Salim Osman (2008). "Indonesian Islamist Party Rebranding Itself before Polls," *Straits Times*, February 9.

Salman Salman (2006). "The Tarbiyah Movement: Why People Join This Indonesian Contemporary Islamic Movement," *Studia Islamika* 13(2): 171–240.

Salwa Ismail (2003). *Rethinking Islamist Politics: Culture, the State and Islamism*. London: I.B. Tauris.

Schwedler, Jillian (2004). "The Islah Party in Yemen," in *Islamic Activism: A Social Movement Theory Approach*, ed. Quintan Wiktorowicz. Bloomington: Indiana University Press, 2004, pp. 205–228.

Schwedler, Jillian (2009). *Faith in Moderation: Islamist Parties in Jordan and Yemen*. Cambridge: Cambridge University Press.

Shadi Hamid and William McCants (eds.) (2017). *Rethinking Political Islam*. New York: Oxford University Press.

Shamsul, A. B. (1997). "Identity Construction, Nation Formation and Islamic Revivalism in Malaysia," in *Islam in an Era of Nation-States: Politics and Religious Renewal in Muslim Southeast Asia*, eds. Robert W. Hefner and Patricia Horvatich. Honolulu: University of Hawaii Press, pp. 207–227.

Sidek Baba (1991). "The Malaysian Study Circle Movement and Some Implications for Educational Development." PhD dissertation, Northern Illinois University.

Siddik Fadil (1989). *Mengangkat Martabat Umat: Koleksi Ucapan Dasar Muktamar Sanawi ABIM*. Kuala Lumpur: Dewan Pustaka Islam.

Singerman, Diane (2004). "The Networked World of Islamist Social Movements," in *Islamic Activism: A Social Movement Theory Approach*, ed. Quintan Wiktorowicz. Bloomington: Indiana University Press, pp. 143–193.

Suharto, Toto (2018). "Transnational Islamic Education in Indonesia: An Ideological Perspective," *Contemporary Islam* 12: 101–122.

Sumanto Al Qurtuby (2018). "Indonesia's Islamist Mobilisation," *Kyoto Review of Southeast Asia* 23. https://kyotoreview.org/issue-23/indonesias-islamist-mobilization/.

Tagliacozzo, Eric (ed.) (2009). *Southeast Asia and the Middle East: Islam, Movement, and the Longue Durée*. Singapore: NUS Press.

Tanuwidjaja, Sunny (2012). "PKS in Post-Reformasi Indonesia: Catching the Catch-All and Moderation Wave," *South East Asia Research* 20(4): 533–549.

Tarrow, Sidney (1996). "States and Opportunities: The Political Structuring of Social Movements," in *Comparative Perspectives on Social Movements*, eds. Doug McAdam, John D. McCarthy, and Mayer N. Zaid. Cambridge: Cambridge University Press, pp. 41–61.

Tilly, Charles (1984). "Social Movements and National Politics," in *State-Making and Social Movements: Essays in History and Theory*, eds. Charles Bright and Susan Harding. Ann Arbor: University of Michigan Press, pp. 297–317.

Times Indonesia (2017). "NU Setuju Penegakan Syariat Islam, Tapi Tegas Menolak Khilafah," *Times Indonesia*, April 26.

Van Bruinessen, Martin (2018). "Indonesian Muslims in a Globalising World: Westernisation, Arabisation, and Indigenising Responses," *RSIS Working Paper* 311, May.

Wahyuddin Halim (2018). "Young Islamic Preachers on Facebook: Pesantren As'adiyah and Its Engagement with Social Media," *Indonesia and the Malay World* 46(134): 44–60.

Walsh, John (2006). "Egypt's Muslim Brotherhood: Understanding Centrist Islam," *Harvard International Review* 24(4): 32–36.

Whittier, Nancy (1995). *Feminist Generations: The Persistence of the Radical Women's Movement*. Philadelphia, PA: Temple University Press.

Wickham, Carrie Rosefsky (2013). *The Muslim Brotherhood: Evolution of an Islamist Movement*. Princeton, NJ: Princeton University Press.

Wiktorowicz, Quintan (2000). *The Management of Islamic Activism: Salafis, the Muslim Brotherhood, and State Power in Jordan*. Buffalo, NY: SUNY Press.

Woltering, Robert (2002). "The Roots of Islamist Popularity," *Third World Quarterly* 23(6): 1133–1143.

Worth, Robert F. (2015). *A Rage for Order: The Middle East in Turmoil, from Tahrir Square to ISIS*. New York: Farrar, Straus, and Giroux.

Yeoh, Seng Guan (2014). "Actually Existing Religious Pluralism in Kuala Lumpur," in *Religious Pluralism, State and Society in Asia*, ed. Chiara Formichi. London: Routledge, pp. 153–171.

Yon Machmudi (2008). *Islamizing Indonesia: The Rise of Jemaah Tarbiyah and the Prosperous Justice Party (PKS)*. Canberra: ANU E-Press.

Yudi Latif (2008). *Indonesian Muslim intelligentsia and Power*. Singapore: Institute of Southeast Asian Studies.

Zainah Anwar (1987). *Islamic Revivalism in Malaysia: Dakwah among the Students*. Petaling Jaya: Pelanduk Publications.

Acknowledgments

I would like to thank Vinay Pathak for research assistance, the two anonymous reviewers for their helpful and constructive comments, and Meredith Weiss for her editorial suggestions.

Politics and Society in Southeast Asia

Edward Aspinall

Australian National University

Edward Aspinall is a professor of politics at the Coral Bell School of Asia-Pacific Affairs, Australian National University. A specialist of Southeast Asia, especially Indonesia, much of his research has focused on democratisation, ethnic politics and civil society in Indonesia and, most recently, clientelism across Southeast Asia.

Meredith L. Weiss

University at Albany, SUNY

Meredith L. Weiss is Professor of Political Science at the University at Albany, SUNY. Her research addresses political mobilization and contention, the politics of identity and development, and electoral politics in Southeast Asia, with particular focus on Malaysia and Singapore.

About the Series

The Elements series Politics and Society in Southeast Asia includes both country-specific and thematic studies on one of the world's most dynamic regions. Each title, written by a leading scholar of that country or theme, combines a succinct, comprehensive, up-to-date overview of debates in the scholarly literature with original analysis and a clear argument.

Cambridge Elements ≡

Politics and Society in Southeast Asia

Printed in the United States
by Baker & Taylor Publisher Services